SIMPLE
PRAYERS
for a
POWERFUL
LIFE

SIMPLE
PRAYERS
for a
POWERFUL
LIFE

TED HAGGARD

Regal

From Gospel Light
Ventura, California, U.S.A.

Published by Regal Books
From Gospel Light
Ventura, California, U.S.A.
Printed in the U.S.A.

Regal Books is a ministry of Gospel Light, an evangelical Christian publisher
dedicated to serving the local church. We believe God's vision for Gospel Light is to
provide church leaders with biblical, user-friendly materials that will help them
evangelize, disciple and minister to children, youth and families.

It is our prayer that this Regal book will help you discover biblical truth for your
own life and help you meet the needs of others. May God richly bless you.

For a free catalog of resources from Regal Books/Gospel Light, please call your Christian
supplier or contact us at 1-800-4-GOSPEL or www.regalbooks.com.

Cover and interior design by Robert Williams
Edited by Rose Decaen

Library of Congress Cataloging-in-Publication Data
Haggard, Ted.
Simple prayers for a powerful life / Ted Haggard.
p. cm.
ISBN 0-8307-3055-9 (trade paper)
1. Prayers. I. Title.

BV245 .H23 2002
242' .8–dc21   2002008620

1 2 3 4 5 6 7 8 9 10 11 12 13 14 15 / 09 08 07 06 05 04 03

Rights for publishing this book in other languages are contracted by Gospel Light Worldwide, the international nonprofit ministry of Gospel Light. Gospel Light Worldwide also
provides publishing and technical assistance to international publishers dedicated to
producing Sunday School and Vacation Bible School curricula and books in the languages of the world. For additional information, visit www.gospellightworldwide.org;
write to Gospel Light Worldwide, P.O. Box 3875, Ventura, CA 93006; or send an e-mail
to info@gospellightworldwide.org.

CONTENTS

Introduction 9

LAUNCHING PRAYERS

Beginning or Renewing a Walk with God

Prayer 1 14
Launching into Eternal Life

Prayer 2 21
Launching into Power

Prayer 3 28
Launching into Health

Prayer 4 36
Launching into Freedom

FLYING PRAYERS

Gaining Freedom and Victory

Prayer 5 44
Flying Free from Other Gods

Prayer 6 48
Flying Free from Judgment

Prayer 7 51
Flying Free from the Occult

Prayer 8 56
Flying Free from Self-Exaltation

Prayer 9 60
Flying Free from Dark Thoughts

Prayer 10 63
Flying Free from Doubt and Unbelief

Prayer 11 66
Flying Free from Negative Spiritual and Emotional Ties

Prayer 12. 69
Flying Free from Occult Bondage and the Effects of Negative Words

Prayer 13 72
Flying Free from Internal Division

Prayer 14 75
Soaring with Freedom

SOARING PRAYERS
Living Daily by the Power of the Holy Spirit

Prayer 15 78
Soaring Through the Door of the Cross

Prayer 16 82
Soaring Through Praying the Scriptures

Prayer 17 86
Soaring Through Praying for Authorities

Prayer 18 90
Soaring Through Prophetic Intercession

Prayer 19 93
Soaring Through Love

Prayer 20 97
Soaring Through Justice

Prayer 21 101
Soaring Through Humility

Prayer 22 104
Soaring Through Authority

Prayer 23 108
Soaring Through Personal Purity

ARRIVING PRAYERS
Going Deeper in the Christian Life

Prayer 24 113
Arriving by Prayer and Fasting

Prayer 25 117
Arriving by Abiding in Him

Introduction

As an associate pastor at Bethany World Prayer Center in Baker, Louisiana, I was responsible for ministering to several inmates in the local parish prison. Since access to them was limited, I had to use written material to coach them in their prayer life. Because so many of them struggled with spiritual darkness, I urged them to pray the prayers from a little booklet my dad had written in order to help people receive deliverance. My dad's booklet, *How to Take Authority over Your Mind, Home, Business and Country,* became so popular with the inmates that I modified it and began encouraging others to use it—with incredible results. Now, after the distribution of over a half million copies of the original, I've modified and expanded it again.

The original booklet was a short, simple leaflet consisting of prayers to pray in order to find freedom from demonic activity and mental confusion. In its first revision, I added the biblical texts and expanded the number of prayers to include the needs of people in general. It was designed so that people could read the prayers aloud and memorize the Bible texts.

Prayer is one of the areas Christians are most curious about, and too many believers don't have the powerful, life-giving prayer life they could have—simply because they don't know where to begin. They don't know how to pray for needs in every area of their life; they don't understand how to access the power of the Holy Spirit to bless their home, family, community and world. But with a few basic tools and ideas, any Christian can have a remarkable and effective prayer life.

Revised again for even greater clarity and depth, the booklet has evolved into *Simple Prayers for a Powerful Life*—a step-by-step guide that allows every believer to walk into overcoming victory.

In order to effectively communicate each step on this journey, I've divided the prayers into four types:

1. **Launching**—The launching prayers are for those who are beginning or renewing a walk with God through the discipline of prayer.
2. **Flying**—The flying prayers are for those gaining freedom.
3. **Soaring**—The soaring prayers can be used repeatedly by mature Christians.
4. **Arriving**—The arriving prayers are to establish a stable, steady victorious Christian life.

Each chapter begins with a prayer, followed by commentary, stories and explanations of how that prayer works. At the end of each chapter, I've listed several verses to show you what the Bible says about these issues and to help you pray God's Word. I suggest you meditate on these verses, so you'll have them ready for use in all your prayer times.

I hope you keep this little book at your bedside, take it with you on retreats, keep it in your briefcase, take it on trips, read it on the bus and use it in group prayer times. The prayers here outline everything you need for having a clean heart, getting over old sins, addressing powers of darkness and generally developing a unique, exciting, dynamic relationship with God. I start with the basics—salvation, finding a relationship with God—and move through to deeper issues in the course of the book.

I can imagine you working your way through this entire book (as I have several times) during a prayer day or weekend prayer retreat, but feel free to focus only on the prayers that apply to you. Not all of these prayers will apply to everyone at every time. You may not have issues with negative emotional ties or the occult, and you may already have a disciplined fasting routine. Either way, it will be helpful to be familiar with all of these types of prayers, so you can use them when issues arise or when ministering to other believers.

Enjoy being empowered to pray simple prayers for a powerful life! May God bless you on your journey!!

LAUNCHING PRAYERS

Beginning or Renewing a
Walk with God

Prayer 1

LAUNCHING INTO ETERNAL LIFE

Heavenly Father, I turn away from my sins and ask You to forgive me. I believe that Jesus Christ is Your Son and that He came to the earth physically in order to destroy the power of darkness in my life. I believe that Jesus paid the price for my sins because He loves me. I ask that the Holy Spirit would come into my heart right now and establish Jesus as Lord of my life. I submit myself to the lordship of Jesus Christ and to the power of the Holy Spirit. I pray that the Holy Spirit would dominate every area of my life and deliver me from the influences of the world that are not of God. I also pray that the Holy Spirit would deliver me from every area of my life that is displeasing to God.

I thank You, Father, for sending Jesus to die on the cross for me. I know that my sins are forgiven because of Christ. I believe You have sent the Holy Spirit into my heart to form me into a new creation. I commit to serve You and to walk in obedience to Your Word for the rest of my life. Thank You for loving me. Thank You for forgiving me. Thank You for hearing my prayer. Thank You for the gift of eternal life. Thank You for giving me the power of the Holy Spirit. Thank You, God! I love You!

I was 16 years old when I first prayed a prayer like this, and it changed my life radically. Like billions of people all over the world, I was trying to find a relationship with God. Unfortunately, for a long time I didn't know that God had already provided a way for my sins to be forgiven and for me to have an intimate personal relationship with Him. I didn't know that all I had to do to receive the life that God has for me was believe that Jesus Christ is the Son of God and submit to the lordship of Christ according to the Scriptures. When I realized how simple and wonderful it was, I was anxious to pray this prayer and begin my new relationship with God. And as soon as I prayed, I could tell that God wanted to speak into my life in a special way. He wanted me to know that we had both a public *and* a private relationship—I was part of His Body (the Church consisting of all believers in Jesus Christ), *and* I was His special child and friend.

God feels that same way about you. You can't pray the prayer above unless God has specifically chosen you to be one of His children. So if you just prayed the prayer above for the first time and meant it with all of your heart, God's forgiveness has just covered all of your sins, His Holy Spirit has come into your heart, and God has begun the process of developing a warm, personal relationship with you.

This relationship will grow because of two eternal truths: the Bible is God's Word, and you can communicate with God personally.

The Bible gives us practical instructions about our personal relationship with God. It teaches us about people, God, angels and other spiritual forces. In addition, it teaches numerous principles about wise living and success. As you read through your Bible, you will find great ideas that will help you in every area of your life. God wants you to be successful. God has a plan for your life. He doesn't want you to be without the information you need to achieve His best plan for every area of your life. The Bible also gives lots of illustrations about our relationship with God by telling the stories of many people who have had a relationship with Him in the past. Some were successful; others were not. These accounts are in the Bible so that we can learn the things that lead to success and be warned about the things that lead to failure. The Bible is full of these stories, and they are by degrees fascinating, challenging and thrilling. Enjoy reading.

But being a follower of Christ is more than just reading the Bible and believing what it teaches. It means living out the dynamic experience of knowing God Himself. I know this might sound a little strange, but even though other Christians will play a very important role in your walk with the Lord, no one else can know Him personally *for you*. This is your friend-ship with God. You can talk to Him just like you would to a friend. You can take private, special time with Him just like you would with a friend. You can tell Him everything. You can share the light, funny things in life as well as the darkest and most intimate things in your life. You can talk to Him, and He will talk to you. How? His primary way of speaking to you is through the Bible. The other way He will speak to you is through His voice in your spirit.

Now this last idea sounds a little strange to many people, and it becomes confusing for too many Christians. God's voice is soft and gentle, and distinguishing His voice from your thoughts takes time. Don't rush in the process of learning to lis-ten for Him. Just take your time, read your Bible, talk to God, and meet with other followers on a regular basis. As you do, there will be occasions when you will hear His voice gently speaking to you. Compare what He's saying with the Bible. Ask some of the older Christians in your church to guide you. As time passes you'll learn to hear the wonderful voice of God in your heart in a beautiful way.

When I gave my life to Christ, I told Him that I wanted a relationship with Him that was unique. Immediately I heard His voice in my heart telling me that I could have a special rela-tionship with Him like no one else had ever had. I knew it was

God's voice. How? I'm not sure. But I knew He was communicating to my heart and that He wanted a personal relationship with me.

That first night after I said the prayer, I told God that I wanted to take the rest of the night and talk with Him. So I went back to my room, knelt by my bed and told God how much I appreciated Him giving me a relationship with Him and forgiving me for all my sins. Then I got into bed and lay there thinking my prayers to God, knowing that He could hear everything I was thinking. It was incredible. As I was thinking my prayers to Him, I would, from time to time, get a thought that I knew was His response back to me. So I lay there until early in the morning enjoying the peace and joy that was in my heart because of this relationship.

God loves you and wants to have this kind of relationship with you. But all of us have a nature inside of us that leans away from genuine godliness. Certainly all people have something within that wants to connect with God—that's why there are so many religions in the world and why people create new religions all the time. But in our basic nature there is also something that wants us to go our own way, do our own thing and worship God (or not worship God) according to our own beliefs.

Human beings have a seemingly limitless capacity to be terrible to one another. The Bible says that all people are separated from God and that the things we do to try to connect with God may make our lives look better, but they don't change us on the inside. But this is what I love about being a follower of Jesus: He changes all of us on the inside. God loves us so much that He takes the old sinful nature that used to dominate every one of us and replaces it with His life, His nature, His character.

That's why the Bible tells us to take off our old selves and to put on Christ (see the list of verses at the end of this chapter). Because of His love for us, God gives us the ability to receive His life in our hearts, which changes the way we live. It's incredible. And because of this, the old way of living doesn't separate us from God any longer. God placed the punishment for our sins on Jesus while He was on the cross, which allows us to receive the power of the perfect life that Jesus lived.

So a miracle occurs when we believe in Jesus. Jesus lived a perfect life but paid the price for our sins. We've lived a sinful life but get the benefits of Jesus' righteousness. When you sincerely prayed the prayer above, the great favor that God felt toward His Son was shared with you. As a result, you received the gift of eternal life. What does that mean?

First of all, it means that your sins are forgiven.

Second, it means that God's Holy Spirit is inside of you, recreating you.

Third, it means that God has a friendly and loving relationship with you. He no longer considers you a sinner, but because of Jesus, He sees you as a perfect person. Wow! Think of that—the God of the universe cares for you and is pleased with you.

Fourth, it means that God's power is working in you. As a result, your life will start to change as you communicate with God and grow in Him. You've met Him now. So if you take advantage of this relationship you've started and don't neglect it, He will powerfully change every area of your life into a life that will be more wonderful than you could ever imagine.

Fifth, it means that as you read your Bible, He will illuminate certain portions and speak into your mind and heart as you learn. It will be more than a book for you. It will be a source of life and joyful instruction.

Sixth, it means that as you develop relationships with other followers of Christ, you will be a blessing to them and they will be a blessing to you. Group worship, prayer, Bible study and close Christian friendships will become increasingly meaningful to you as you grow in your relationship with God.

Seventh, when you die, you will go to heaven. Because of Christ's work on the cross for you and your response to that work, you will never have your sins held against you. You are forgiven. You have the nature of God inside you. You are submitted to the Bible as the Word of God. You have turned from your old ways and habits and have decided to let your life be dominated by God's will. Those who die to their old way of life because of their belief in Jesus have absolute assurance that when they die they will go to heaven. You don't have to earn it. Jesus did it for you. But you do have to reject being your own boss, turn your life toward God and receive what He has for you. As you do that, His work becomes effective in your life. Congratulations!

Now, go back to the prayer and pray through it again. Receive what the Lord has for you. And as you sincerely pray this prayer with your heart, I want to be the first to welcome you into the kingdom of God!

*P*RAYING GOD'S WORD

I tell you the truth, he who believes has everlasting life (John 6:47).

And we know that in all things God works for the good of those who love him, who have been called according to his purpose. For those God foreknew he also predestined to be conformed to the likeness of his Son, that he might be the firstborn among many brothers. And those he predestined, he also called; those he called, he also justified; those he justified, he also glorified (Rom. 8:28-30).

Therefore, if anyone is in Christ, he is a new creation; the old has gone, the new has come! (2 Cor. 5:17).

Therefore [Jesus] is able to save completely those who come to God through him, because he always lives to intercede for them (Heb. 7:25).

Praise be to the God and Father of our Lord Jesus Christ! In his great mercy he has given us new birth into a living hope through the resurrection of Jesus Christ from the dead (1 Pet. 1:3).

LAUNCHING INTO POWER

Heavenly Father, I am thirsty. I want the fruit and gifts of the Holy Spirit in my life. Please fill me with the Holy Spirit. Just as many are baptized in water in response to their commitment to You, I now want to be baptized in the Holy Spirit. You have guaranteed me salvation and I have experienced the work of the Spirit in my life in a special way, and I want more. I want to be filled with the Holy Spirit. I want to be dipped in the Holy Spirit. I want to be immersed in the Holy Spirit. I want to overflow with the life of the Spirit.

I want the fruit of the Spirit to become common in my life. I pray for love, joy, peace, patience, kindness, goodness, faithfulness, gentleness and self-control. I also want the gifts of the Holy Spirit in my life. I ask You to give me the gifts of wisdom, knowledge, faith, healing, miracles, prophecy, discernment, tongues and interpretation. I ask You to work all of Your gifts and all of the fruit of the Holy Spirit into my life.

Thank You for baptizing me in Your Spirit, for giving me the gifts of the Holy Spirit and for working the fruit of the Spirit into my life. I am grateful for Your power that lives in me.

I was in college when I prayed a prayer like this for the first time, and it launched me into a unique ability to demonstrate the power of God to those around me. All of us receive the Holy Spirit when we repent of our sins and submit to Christ as our

Lord and Savior. But something incredibly powerful happens when we ask God to manifest the power of His Holy Spirit in our lives in the form of His fruit and gifts.

What happens? What does it mean to be baptized in the Holy Spirit? There is wide-ranging debate on this topic throughout the Church, and unfortunately it has been the source of much contention. However, if we look directly at what the Bible has to say about these issues, it really is quite simple. Of course, it is fairly easy to explain the fruit of the Holy Spirit—all believers agree that the Holy Spirit helps us grow in love, joy, peace, patience and so on (see Gal. 5:22-23), and everyday Christian life consists of manifesting those attributes. But I'd like to explain the baptism in the Holy Spirit and the manifestation of spiritual gifts so that you'll be completely free to grow in the gifts of the Holy Spirit with confidence and understanding.

John 20:19-23 records Jesus' first meeting with the disciples after His resurrection. In verse 22, Jesus "breathes" on them and says, "Receive the Holy Spirit." At that moment, when the disciples received the Holy Spirit and believed in Jesus' death and resurrection, they were in exactly the same position spiritually that we are when we ask Jesus to come into our hearts: born again with the Holy Spirit dwelling inside them.

But later, Jesus tells the disciples not to leave Jerusalem until they receive the gift that was promised by God the Father. He says, "For John baptized with water, but in a few days you will be baptized with the Holy Spirit" (Acts 1:5). In other words, though these followers knew Jesus personally, had their names written in the Lamb's Book of Life (see Luke 10:20) and already had the Holy Spirit (see John 20:22) they still needed to experience the baptism of the Holy Spirit—they needed to have their spirits immersed in God's Spirit just as John had immersed people in water.

Why did they need this? Because they would not have the power to fulfill God's perfect plan without it. Jesus told them,

"But you will receive power when the Holy Spirit comes on you; and you will be my witnesses in Jerusalem, and in all Judea and Samaria, and to the ends of the earth" (Acts 1:8). The power of God was going to intensify greatly in the disciples' lives once the Holy Spirit came on them in this special way, and Jesus was directly telling His followers to receive this power before they went forward in their lives and ministry.

This is why I consider being filled with the Holy Spirit a fundamental part of beginning your life in Christ. Without His power, your life might be filled with unnecessary struggles and weaknesses. But when God gives you His own strength, you will have stronger tools to win spiritual battles and be a witness for Him.

With the baptism in the Holy Spirit comes the ability to operate in the gifts of the Holy Spirit, which very often includes a prayer language, or "tongues." In Acts 2:4, when the first group of believers were baptized in the Holy Spirit, the Bible says that all of them were "filled with the Holy Spirit and began to speak in other tongues as the Spirit enabled them."

What were those tongues? They were different types of spoken languages, both human and nonhuman. It is clear that the disciples were miraculously speaking in languages from all over the world because people from different countries all heard their own language being spoken (see Acts 2:11). This still happens today: Christian missionaries sometimes report occasions when they are suddenly given the ability to communicate in a foreign language. Additionally, though, those who are baptized in the Holy Spirit can speak in a kind of angelic prayer language.

In 1 Corinthians 13:1, Paul writes, "If I speak in the tongues of men and of angels, but have not love, I am only a resounding gong or a clanging cymbal." Paul mentions both types here— tongues of men and tongues of angels. Later in the same letter he writes, "For anyone who speaks in a tongue does not speak to men but to God. Indeed, no one understands him; he utters mysteries with his spirit" (1 Cor. 14:2). All of this reinforces what Paul says in Romans 8:26-27:

> In the same way, the Spirit helps us in our weakness. We do not know what we ought to pray for, but the Spirit himself intercedes for us with groans that words cannot express. And he who searches our hearts knows the mind of the Spirit, because the Spirit intercedes for the saints in accordance with God's will.

In other words, the Bible is saying that the Spirit will pray God's perfect will through us. Why? Because we don't know what we ought to pray in every situation. So God sends his Spirit into our hearts to pray His perfect will through us. This is incredible, but it does make sense; it is yet another way that we are tools for God to use here on Earth to accomplish His work.

Whether we speak in tongues of men or angels, however, the gift of tongues is definitely a language that comes from the Holy Spirit, and it is one of the primary ways believers are strengthened in Christ. First Corinthians 14:4 begins, "He who speaks in a tongue edifies himself." Interestingly, this is the only place in the New Testament where it specifically says what believers need to do to build themselves up spiritually. We know that there are other ways to build ourselves up spiritually, such as Bible reading, fellowship with other Christians, living a holy lifestyle and attending life-giving believers' meetings. But when the Bible comments specifically about building ourselves up, it encourages us to speak in tongues.

No doubt, there is protocol in the operation of all gifts, including these two. There is a required protocol associated with everything in life. Electricity can be misused, but we still use it and are careful in doing so because we want its benefits. The same principle is at work with the gifts and the fruit of the

Spirit. They can be misused, but they are so beneficial that the Bible commands that we "eagerly desire spiritual gifts" (1 Cor. 14:1); so I believe it is worth working through the difficulties in order to enjoy the life and power of God.

Many people overemphasize tongues because they feel it is the only initial sign of baptism in the Holy Spirit. I don't believe that, and I don't believe that everyone who is baptized in the Holy Spirit will necessarily receive a prayer language. But I believe tongues is an extremely important gift and that we should eagerly desire it, just as we should the other gifts—as Jesus suggested, we need them all in order to be effective witnesses to those around us.

Many of us have been taught that tongues and the other gifts ceased many years ago. Not so. Actually, there is no biblical teaching that says that, nor is there any historical evidence to validate that notion. The only way people can teach that is to draw Scriptures out of context and distort them. I'll give you one example and then I think you'll understand.

Many theologians use a set of verses in 1 Corinthians 13 to teach that tongues are no longer operational in the church. First Corinthians 13:8-10 says, "Love never fails. But where there are prophecies, they will cease; where there are tongues, they will be stilled; where there is knowledge, it will pass away. For we know in part and we prophesy in part, but when perfection comes, the imperfect disappears." When some Bible scholars read these verses, they assume that perfection has already come, either through the formation of the Church or the completion of the Bible. Thus, they say that tongues have been stilled, and prophecy has ceased. But as you can see, the verses themselves do not allude to either the Church or the Bible. And oddly, these theologians never comment on knowledge, which obviously has not ceased. We do know in part, and we still prophesy in part. Obviously, we have not achieved perfection, and these theologians have no basis for arbitrarily assigning Paul's idea here to the Bible or the formation of the Church.

Prophecy, tongues and knowledge as we know them will pass away at the second coming of the Lord Jesus. Why? Because we will be with Him. We won't need to prophesy, pray in tongues or turn to human knowledge for answers: "Now we see but a poor reflection as in a mirror; then we shall see face to face" (1 Cor. 13:12). Who will we see face-to-face? Jesus Christ.

This and other equally weak "proof texts" of the demise of the gifts of the Spirit in the modern Church do not give any Bible-believing person reason to think that the gifts are not fully available to all Christians today. If we ask, seek and knock, we will receive, find and have the doors open to us.

Okay, now you have it. Be filled with the Holy Spirit! Earnestly desire everything God has for you, and He will gladly give to you.

℘raying God's Word

Now about spiritual gifts, brothers, I do not want you to be ignorant (1 Cor. 12:1).

Now to each one the manifestation of the Spirit is given for the common good. To one there is given through the Spirit the message of wisdom, to another the message of knowledge by means of the same Spirit, to another faith by the same Spirit, to another gifts of healing by that one Spirit, to another miraculous powers, to another prophecy, to another distinguishing between spirits, to another speaking in different kinds of tongues, and to still another the interpretation of tongues. All these are the work of one and the same Spirit, and he gives them to each one, just as he determines (1 Cor. 12:7-11).

Follow the way of love and eagerly desire the spiritual gifts, especially the gift of prophecy (1 Cor. 14:1).

For John baptized with water, but in a few days you will be baptized with the Holy Spirit. But you will receive power when the Holy Spirit comes on you; and you will be my witnesses in Jerusalem, and in all Judea and Samaria, and to the ends of the earth (Acts 1:5,8).

So I say, live by the Spirit, and you will not gratify the desires of the sinful nature (Gal. 5:16).

The fruit of the Spirit is love, joy, peace, patience, kindness, goodness, faithfulness, gentleness and self-control. Against such things there is no law (Gal. 5:22-23).

LAUNCHING INTO HEALTH

Heavenly Father, I thank You that my body was fearfully and wonderfully made. Thank You for my height, hair color and skin. Thank You that Your Holy Spirit lives in my body, making it a temple of the Spirit.

Because You have chosen to live in me, I know that my body is important to You. I confess that I have misused and neglected it. I repent of using my body for selfishness and for subjecting my body to an unhealthy lifestyle. Father, forgive me for taking my body for granted and for not being adequately grateful for it.

I know that You hate disease and that You want my body healthy and strong, so I can fulfill Your perfect plan for my life. So in Jesus' name, I claim the healing that was provided for me through the wounds of the Lord Jesus Christ. I command every cell in my body to line up with the Word of God and be healed. I pray that You would heal every member of my body so that every system in my body would work perfectly.

In Jesus' name I command every evil spirit that is trying to create disease or has created disease in my body to depart. I break the power of every demonic force in my life and command that my body function perfectly as designed by God. I refuse the powers of darkness any access to my body; I deny every word ever spoken against my health; I break the power of any witch-craft performed against me in order to destroy my health.

Heavenly Father, if there is any part of my body that needs a creative miracle of healing, I pray that You would do it now. Extend Your mercy powerfully toward me, Lord. You are the creator of all, and You can create new cells, organs, bones, cartilage, muscles and nerves in my body. Heal me now in Jesus' name.

Thank You that You want me well. Father, I know that Jesus was beaten and bruised for my healing, so I thank You now for my healing.

The psalmist David wrote matchlessly powerful and insightful words about God's involvement in the formation of our bodies. Psalm 139:13-16 says,

For you created my inmost being; you knit me together in my mother's womb. I praise you because I am fearfully and wonderfully made; your works are wonderful, I know that full well. My frame was not hidden from you when I was made in the secret place. When I was woven together in the depths of the earth, your eyes saw my unformed body. All the days ordained for me were written in your book before one of them came to be.

These verses speak volumes to me; they encourage me to accept the way that God made me and appreciate that my body is not simply a product of random biology. My body is part of the plan of God for my life, so I thank God for the way He created me and I am grateful and content with God's work in giving me the body that I have.

The above prayer lays the proper foundation for our relationship with God with respect to our bodies. We have to understand that our bodies are important to Him because it is through our bodies that we fulfill God's plan for our lives. If we harm our bodies or if they don't function well, then we are limited in the amount of things we can do for Him. That's why God wants our bodies to be whole. So we must recognize our responsibility to eat correctly, to exercise and to maintain our bodies for His glory.

The prayer addresses the two primary sources of sickness and disease: demonic activity and physical problems. Not all sickness is a mere physical problem; sometimes a sick person is being affected by spirits of darkness. In Luke 4, Jesus heals Simon's mother-in-law, who was suffering from a high fever. The Bible says, "So he bent over her and rebuked the fever, and it left her. She got up at once and began to wait on them" (v. 39). Can fever hear? Not if it is simply a physical ailment. But if it has a spiritual cause, it can indeed hear and can leave when commanded. Jesus treated this problem as if the fever were a force of darkness harming Simon's mother-in-law. Likewise, Luke later tells about a woman "who had been crippled by a spirit for eighteen years" (13:11). Jesus heals this woman through laying His hands on her, and she is immediately able to stand up and praise God (see 13:13).

Sometimes, then, when we're dealing with a physical ailment, we're dealing with demonic issues. At other times, people are sick because of entirely physical problems, and we should pray for creative miracles in their bodies. (We cannot always tell the difference between the two, but often God gives us discernment to know if a problem is uniquely physical or demonic.) No matter what our health problem, we can ask God to perform miracles in our bodies, to restore our bodies supernaturally, so we can function as He originally intended.

Does God want to do miracles? Certainly He does. Don't let people convince you that God wants you to be sick. It's not true. The apostle Peter wrote, "[Jesus] himself bore our sins in his body on the tree, so that we might die to sins and live for righteousness; by his wounds you have been healed" (1 Pet. 2:24). See, He forgives us and gives us the power to live in His righteousness—and He wants us healthy!

Both the Old and New Testaments contain accounts of God performing miracles to heal people's bodies. In 2 Kings 4:32-35, for instance, Elisha prays for a dead boy and God heals him:

> When Elisha reached the house, there was the boy lying dead on his couch. He went in, shut the door on the two of them [the boy's mother and Elisha's servant] and prayed to the LORD. Then he got on the bed and lay upon the boy, mouth to mouth, eyes to eyes, hands to hands. As he stretched himself out upon him, the boy's body grew warm. Elisha turned away and walked back and forth in the room and then got on the bed and stretched out upon him once more. The boy sneezed seven times and opened his eyes.

And of course, Jesus performs many healings that are recounted in the Gospels. Most believers are familiar with the story of the leper who was made whole by Christ.

> When [Jesus] came down from the mountainside, large crowds followed him. A man with leprosy came and knelt before him and said, "Lord, if you are willing, you can make me clean." Jesus reached out his hand and touched the man. "I am willing," he said, "Be clean!" Immediately he was cured of his leprosy (Matt. 8:1-3).

These and other accounts throughout Scripture reveal God's desire to heal us. Does everyone get healed? No. Why not? Because we are on Earth. In heaven, where God's perfect will is fully manifested, there will be no sickness, disease, handicap, deformity or ailment. But here on Earth, we receive healing to the degree that the kingdom of God is manifested around us.

This is a very personal subject for me because I have a son who is handicapped. When he was born, the doctors said he would not walk, run or play normally with others. To this day, he's not normal. But he does walk, run and play with friends. How? Well, I believe that God is working in his life in a beautiful way. Why is he still sick? Because his genetic makeup is not right because he is a member of the human race. Will he ever be normal? Yes, he will be 100 percent whole in heaven, but we're not sure whether he will be 100 percent normal while on Earth. Is it God's will for him to be normal? Yes, it is. But it is also God's will for everyone on Earth to come to Christ. How do we reconcile the difference between what God wants and what is happening around us? We just stay steady. We continue to pray and work for everyone on Earth to come to Christ, and we continue to pray and work for my son to be completely whole. We pray, we do everything we can, and then we trust God with complete contentment.

But I know the question persists, especially for those of us who have experienced severe sickness, either in our own bodies or in that of our loved ones. Since God wants people well and He is sovereign, why isn't everyone healed?

Well, God's will is not the only factor impacting our lives. There are a variety of forces at work on Earth:

1. **God's perfect will**—Jesus taught us to pray, "Thy Kingdom come. Thy will be done in earth, as it is in heaven" (Matt. 6:10, *KJV*). In heaven, God's perfect will is being done right now. There is no disease, no death, no unbelief. But here on Earth, we receive small portions of His kingdom in our hearts through the Holy Spirit and see His perfect will manifested from time to time. Earth is not heaven.

2. **The influences of darkness**—The Bible calls the devil "the god of this world" (2 Cor. 4:4, *KJV*). Why? Because

even though the devil is defeated, the majority of people in the world serve him (whether they know it or not); they identify with him because of their old sinful nature and their love of the knowledge of good and evil. The devil and his demons are real; they try to influence people and, if allowed, they can actually enter people to perform their evil deeds through them. That's why we encourage people to be filled with the Holy Spirit, submit to God's Word and become connected to other believers in a local church. That is the only way to overcome the influence of darkness in our lives.

3. **The influences of our old sinful nature**—All people have a basic human nature that tends toward disobedience. That's why parents struggle to train their kids to love and to share, and it's why we work to resist our own tendencies to be arrogant, greedy and immoral. In heaven, the old sinful nature will be eliminated; there, God's good nature will prevail in all of us all of the time. But while we're here, there is a daily struggle between the domination of the Holy Spirit and obedience to God's Word and the desire for our old sinful nature to be in control and open the door to darkness. This is why we're commanded in Scripture to constantly be filled with the Holy Spirit and to renew our minds consistently by reading the Scriptures.

4. **The laws of nature**—All of us know that if we eat junk food and watch TV all day, we will be sick, depressed and drained. That's natural law at work. Physical laws rule here on Earth, so if we contract a virus, that virus is going to have to be dealt with in order for us to be well again—even though it's not God's plan that we be sick. If we misuse our bodies, the natural consequence will be that our bodies will weaken and eventually fail.

Certainly, from time to time, God will override the physical laws of the universe. When He does, we call that a miracle. We all appreciate miracles, but in heaven, we won't need these miracles. Why? Because in heaven His perfect will prevails.

5. **The impact of bad ideas**—Here on Earth there are systems of thought that paralyze people and cause them to make horrible mistakes with their lives. In heaven, truth will be evident and bad ideas will be nonexistent. But here, we have to sort through the difference between good advice and foolishness. Many people ruin their lives and even have their lives cut short contrary to God's perfect plan because they believed the wrong set of ideas.

So what should we do? We pray for God's will to be done, we resist darkness and the sinful nature and bad ideas, and we pray for God to revoke natural law when necessary. And we trust Him no matter what. Mostly, we need to believe that God's perfect will is that we be whole. We need to embrace the full power of salvation, be filled with the Holy Spirit and commit ourselves to be as healthy and strong as God planned for us to be. Now, repeat the prayer at the opening of this chapter and then go on to the final chapter in the launching section of this book.

PRAYING GOD'S WORD

Praise the LORD, . . . who forgives all your sins and heals all your diseases (Ps. 103:2-3).

For you created my inmost being; you knit me together in my mother's womb. I praise you because I am fearfully and wonderfully made; your works are wonderful, I know that full well. My frame was not hidden from you when I was made in the secret place. When I was woven together in the depths of the earth, your eyes saw my unformed body. All the days ordained for me were written in your book before one of them came to be (Ps. 139:13-16).

But he was pierced for our transgressions, he was crushed for our iniquities; the punishment that brought us peace was upon him, and by his wounds we are healed (Isa. 53:5).

Those troubled by evil spirits were cured, and the people all tried to touch him, because power was coming from him and healing them all (Luke 6:18-19).

[Lord,] stretch out your hand to heal and perform miraculous signs and wonders through the name of your holy servant Jesus (Acts 4:30).

LAUNCHING INTO FREEDOM

In the name of the Lord Jesus Christ, I command my old sinful nature to die. I want my life to be saturated with the Holy Spirit and submitted to the Word of God. My body is the temple of the Holy Spirit, my mind is being renewed daily with the Scriptures, and my life is being strengthened through healthy relationships with other believers. I don't want to live for myself, for the world or under the influence of darkness. I am committed to live the life that God designed for me.

I renounce every evil spirit that is trying to work in, through or around me. In Jesus' name, I command every dark spirit away from me, and I proclaim that the powers of darkness have no grounds to be in or around my life. I am committed to the lordship of Christ, which means no other influence can dominate me.

Lord, deliver me from the evil one. Thank You.

There are several types of spirits in the world. You are a spirit, and you express yourself through your body. The Holy Spirit is a spirit, and He dwells inside of people and manifests Himself through spiritual gifts and fruit. Angels are also spirits, and though we have no biblical accounts of angels inhabiting bodies, we do know they minister to people and can influence their decisions. Demons are also spirits, and like other spiritual beings, demons minister to people and try to impact their lives.

When Jesus taught His disciples how to pray, He instructed them to pray against evil spirits specifically: "And lead us not into temptation, but deliver us from the evil one" (Matt. 6:13). Jesus thought part of everyday prayer was praying for protection against the work of demonic forces.

But how do we *really* do it? How do we pray against demons, especially concerning our own lives?

The prayer above addresses evil spirits that are "in, through or around" the person praying. Why? Because there has long been confusion among Christians about how demons work and whether they can work through us at all. Some people adamantly claim that evil spirits can work inside of Christians, through possession. Others argue that demons can merely stir thoughts inside a Christian's head but cannot actually possess his or her body. Still others maintain that demons are allowed neither to enter bodies nor to influence thoughts but can only impact one's surrounding environment.

Essentially, I believe these arguments are beside the point. There is no biblical or practical reason to believe (as some do) that Christians are automatically delivered from evil spirits upon salvation, that evil spirits are not allowed to enter or impact believers or that the baptism in the Holy Spirit removes all traces of evil in the believer's life. However, it is very clear from the Bible that Jesus and His disciples believed evil spirits were at work in people's lives and that the early Christians had to contend with demonic forces. Thus, we should concentrate on doing the work of praying against evil, not debating how evil works.

Paul said he had a thorn in the flesh that was a messenger of Satan. Was it inside his body or outside? I don't know and I don't care. What I do know is that we are commanded to cast demons out and set people free. When someone is clearly dealing with a demonic issue, I never analyze the location of the demons. I spend my energy on fighting for the person's freedom.

In Matthew 12:43-45, Jesus delivers a strong exhortation to be filled with the Holy Spirit and the Word of God:

> When an evil spirit comes out of a man, it goes through arid places seeking rest and does not find it. Then it says, "I will return to the house I left." When it arrives, it finds the house unoccupied, swept clean and put in order. Then it goes and takes with it seven other spirits more wicked than itself, and they go in and live there. And the final condition of that man is worse than the first. That is how it will be with this wicked generation.

It is clear here that evil spirits want to inhabit people's lives as they would inhabit a house. Whether this is referring to actual possession or not, it is certain that we need to be saved, filled with the Holy Spirit, healed in our bodies and delivered in order to launch into the life that Christ has for us.

Fortunately, the devil is already defeated. He may have influence in our world today, but his story is one of continual humiliation and defeat. The devil's first humiliation is recorded in Genesis 3:14-15 as God curses the serpent, who represents Satan, after he successfully deceives Eve:

> Cursed are you above all the livestock and all the wild animals! You will crawl on your belly and you will eat dust all the days of your life. And I will put enmity between you and the woman, and between your offspring and hers; he will crush your head, and you will strike his heel.

Of course, the devil was firmly and finally defeated when Jesus died on the cross. Jesus' death completed the work of redemption, opening the door for everyone to have the power and glory that Satan wants. The Cross gave people the ability to become children of God, to receive His righteousness and to represent Him here on Earth. Paul's letter to the church at Colosse puts it this way: "And having disarmed the powers and authorities, [Jesus] made a public spectacle of them, triumphing over them by the cross" (Col. 2:15).

When Jesus overcame the forces and powers of Satan through His death, He also made it possible for us to share in His triumph. Everyone who believes in Jesus' work on the cross automatically enters into God's victory. They gain eternal access into the winning side of the battle, and they gain power to wage war against demonic forces.

However, there is a paradox: Demons are defeated through Jesus' work on the cross, yet demons continue to influence people's lives and manifest themselves in terrible ways (notice the last part of God's curse on Satan quoted above, which points towards the continual battle between humans and the devil). This is similar to our discussion earlier about sickness and healing—God wants us to be well, but we can still become sick. But just as we have to stay steady in times of illness, we must remain constantly vigilant in working against the powers of darkness. As Paul wrote to the Christians in Ephesus, "For our struggle is not against flesh and blood, but against the rulers, against the authorities, against the powers of this dark world and against the spiritual forces of evil in the heavenly realms" (Eph. 6:12). There is an ongoing battle, and though the victory is Christ's now and forevermore because He is always and everywhere more powerful than Satan, we still must stand against the enemy.

Demons are incredibly deceptive. They are wily and crafty, particularly when it comes to influencing people's thoughts. They can masquerade as God, a departed loved one or even as the person they are trying to influence. Many people think they are communicating with God when they are actually in contact with demonic activity. Others think they have discovered the secrets to communication with the dead, when in reality they are communicating with demonic spirits. Some people under demonic attacks hate themselves passionately, cannot control their sin or develop a mental illness.

This is not to say that all mental illnesses are demonic or that the sinful nature does not work without demonic activity. Some mental illnesses are just physical problems, and some sin issues do not have anything to do with demons. But it is important to consider and confront demonic activity when people are debilitated with such issues, because demons work in cunning ways. When it comes to sin, demonic activity can compound what is already a very tricky problem. Evil spirits can be triggered into power because of the old sinful nature and, once entrenched, they hold on with vengeance.

So what do we do? We cast them out. We negate their power. We force them to leave. Jesus says in Matthew 11:12, "From the days of John the Baptist until now, the kingdom of heaven has been forcefully advancing, and forceful men lay hold of it." It takes force, continual and bold resistance against the power of demons, to advance God's kingdom.

Think about this. Remember it. Believe it. Too many Christians don't bother to pray against demonic forces. They think of demons as archaic or too fantastic or a product of people's imaginations. But they're not. They are real, and they'd love for us to act as if they don't exist. We have to follow the example of Jesus and confront evil forces directly. We cannot be cowed. We cannot act as if we are too intelligent or sophisticated to think about such things. We must go to war. We must fight in Jesus' name.

And we must look to the Word of God, which gives us a powerful strategy for battling against demonic forces in our everyday lives.

Put on the full armor of God so that you can take your stand against the devil's schemes. [And] so that when the day of evil comes, you may be able to stand your ground, and after you have done everything, to stand. Stand firm then, with the belt of truth buckled around your waist, with the breastplate of righteousness in place, and with your feet fitted with the readiness that comes from the gospel of peace. In addition to all this, take up the shield of faith, with which you can extinguish all the flaming arrows of the evil one. Take the helmet of salvation and the sword of the Spirit, which is the word of God. And pray in the Spirit on all occasions with all kinds of prayers and requests. With this in mind, be alert and always keep on praying for all the saints (Eph. 6:11,13-18).

Clearly, this entire passage is a call to battle, from the encouragement to put on our armor to the admonition to stay alert. We need to put on our armor and forcefully confront the powers of darkness that want to wage war on ourselves, our families, our churches, our businesses, our cities and our country.

One more thing to keep in mind: 2 Corinthians 2:11 says that we need to forgive "in order that Satan might not outwit us. For we are not unaware of his schemes." If we harbor unforgiveness, we can open a door for demonic activity. Be sure to read the section on praying against judgment in order to deal effectively with this area in your heart.

Now, pray the prayer at the beginning of this section one more time, and as you do, you'll win.

PRAYING GOD'S WORD

The people were all so amazed that they asked each other, "What is this? A new teaching—and with authority! He even gives orders to evil spirits and they obey him" (Mark 1:27).

If you forgive anyone, I also forgive him. And what I have forgiven—if there was anything to forgive—I have forgiven in the sight of Christ for your sake, in order that Satan might not outwit us. For we are not unaware of his schemes (2 Cor. 2:10-11).

It is for freedom that Christ has set us free (Gal. 5:1).

And his incomparably great power [is] for us who believe (Eph. 1:19).

Finally, be strong in the Lord and in his mighty power. Put on the full armor of God so that you can take your stand against the devil's schemes (Eph. 6:10-11).

FLYING PRAYERS

*Gaining Freedom
and Victory*

FLYING FREE FROM OTHER GODS

Heavenly Father, I believe You are the one true God. I believe You are the invisible God of Abraham, Isaac and Jacob. I believe that Jesus Christ is Your Son, the Messiah, and that He came in the flesh to destroy the works of the devil.

Lord Jesus, You died on the cross for my sins and rose from the dead on the third day. I confess my sins and repent. Thank You for redeeming me, cleansing me, justifying me and sanctifying me in Your blood. You are the only God who loves me; You are the only God I trust; You are the only God I want to serve.

There is only one true God, but there are many spiritual beings that want to be God and pretend to be God. The Bible refers to the devil as the god of this world (see 2 Cor. 4:4, *KJV*), and certainly there are many other spiritual forces at work throughout creation. Further, some people choose to put their faith in these forces. Sometimes you will notice that certain gods, or spirits, hold sway over a particular region, exercising influence over the people of that region. These spirits will work to convince people that they are God. But the Bible forbids us from worshiping any god other than the one creator of the universe, whose Son is Jesus—which is why Christian missionaries spend their lives trying to help people see that there is really only one God worth serving.

The one true God is invisible. He is a spirit, and there are no human symbols, statues, pictures or buildings that reflect Him perfectly. Because He is a spirit, He communicates to people through His Holy Spirit and receives worship by the Spirit. This is very mysterious and difficult for us to understand, which is why God sent His Son. Jesus is the perfect reflection of God; He is the image of God in the form of a man. When we read Matthew, Mark, Luke and John in the New Testament, we learn how God deals with people and how He expresses Himself. The miraculous signs and wonders that constantly accompanied Jesus were proof that He controlled creation, and His death and resurrection fulfilled the promises God had made to Israel to send a Messiah to redeem humankind. This was—and is—the one God, and the only appropriate response on our part is to believe in Him.

So in the prayer above, we confess who God is in contrast to the other spiritual forces who try to attract our allegiances, and then we receive with thanksgiving four powerful provisions from God: redemption, cleansing, justification and sanctification. Let's look at each of these briefly.

Redemption—When we thank God for redeeming us, we are thanking Him for purchasing us. You are costly to God—your life is valuable to Him. He gave His Son in order to purchase you out of sin, the world and death. You are now God's property. Because of this, you can stand confidently knowing that the world, the old sinful nature and the devil have no claim on you. You have life. You belong to God!

Cleansing—God not only covers our sins with His blood, but He also digs deep into our lives and cleanses out the crud, dirt and grime. He cleanses our minds, our bodies and our spirits from darkness and death. If there are areas in your life that are displeasing to God, ask Him to begin the process of cleaning these things out. This is very important: He doesn't just cover us—He also cleanses us.

Justification—The best phrase I know to communicate the idea behind this term is a little play on the word itself: When I am justified in Christ, it is *just-as-if-I'd* never sinned. In other words, our sins become placed upon Him on the cross, which opens the door for His righteousness to be placed in us today. So when you pray, worship or resist temptation, you can do it with confidence because in Christ you are just as if you'd never sinned.

Sanctification—When something is sanctified, it is set apart for a specific purpose. You, too, are sanctified, which means you have been called by God—called to break away from the values and lifestyles that dominate so many in the world. You are called to be holy. Frankly, this means you'll be abnormal, different, unusual and contrary to many of the routine standards of the world, but that's exactly how God wants you to be. Just as fine china is kept separate from common dishes, so your life has been set apart for God.

Now, pray the above prayer again; then proceed to the next prayer.

PRAYING GOD'S WORD

You shall have no other gods before me (Exod. 20:3).

Have mercy on me, O God, according to your unfailing love; according to your great compassion blot out my transgressions. Wash away all my iniquity and cleanse me from my sin (Ps. 51:1-2).

For all have sinned and fall short of the glory of God, and are justified freely by his grace through the redemption that came by Christ Jesus (Rom. 3:23-24).

You were washed, you were sanctified, you were justified in the name of the Lord Jesus Christ and by the Spirit of our God (1 Cor. 6:11).

For you know that it was not with perishable things such as silver or gold that you were redeemed from the empty way of life handed down to you from your forefathers, but with the precious blood of Christ, a lamb without blemish or defect. He was chosen before the creation of the world, but was revealed in these last times for your sake (1 Pet. 1:18-20).

Prayer 6

FLYING FREE FROM
JUDGMENT

*Heavenly Father, I have a confession to make. I have not loved
but have resented certain people and have harbored unforgiveness toward them in my heart. I call upon You, Lord, to help me
forgive them. I do now forgive (name them, both living and
dead). I ask You to forgive them, too. Also, I forgive myself in the
name of Jesus Christ.*

Take time with this short prayer. Go through it over and over
again as people come to mind, and do it regularly. Ask the Lord
to remind you of anyone or anything that you might need to forgive. Think back as far as you can, and be humble. Remember
the verse discussed earlier: 2 Corinthians 2:11 says that we
should forgive in order to ensure that Satan cannot trick us.
Forgiveness is extremely powerful, but unforgiveness is powerful
as well. We need to cleanse ourselves of all unforgiveness and
resentfulness by refusing to judge others any longer and forgiving them as Jesus has forgiven us.

Forgiving those who have wronged you does not mean that
you agree with them or that you are approving what they have
done. It just means that you are not going to hold anything
against them. You may not completely forget, but if you forgive
them, you release the passion and negative feelings associated
with the memory of the incident.

I believe that forgiveness is the single most significant element in maintaining a clean heart and a powerful personal life. Leviticus 19:18 says, "Do not seek revenge or bear a grudge against one of your people, but love your neighbor as yourself." Jesus put it even more directly: "For if you forgive men when they sin against you, your heavenly Father will also forgive you. But if you do not forgive men their sins, your Father will not forgive your sins" (Matt. 6:14-15). God wants to be your heavenly Father. If someone hurts you, He wants to be the one to defend you. He wants you to forgive them, and when you do, it opens the door for His forgiveness to be effective in your heart.

Every month or so I take time during prayer and ask the Lord to remind me of anyone or anything that I need to forgive. When I do this, I verbally forgive every person or thing that comes to my mind. It's always amazing to me how many people I need to forgive, and interestingly enough, many of them are people I didn't realize I had anything against. That's the way our hearts work. Very often we develop a little disappointment, wound or grievance that does not even register in our minds. If we don't deal with it, the consequences can be terrible.

Should we confront people who have hurt us? Yes, it's fine to have confrontations, but we must be careful to do it when our hearts are clean and when we no longer hold any resentment.

Do we forgive even if they haven't asked for forgiveness? Yes, we do. Why? Because giving forgiveness is what we need to do for our hearts to be clean. If they are humble and ask for forgiveness, that's wonderful; but we need to give forgiveness unconditionally—regardless of what they do—for our own protection. If we don't, their violation continues to have a hook inside our hearts and it could unnecessarily hurt us for years to come.

Don't forget to forgive yourself. You have failed yourself and others in many areas. Make sure you don't have a list of grievances you are holding against yourself.

One last thing: You might need to forgive God. Sounds strange, doesn't it? God is perfect, and He doesn't need your forgiveness. But you might have had some disappointment in your life that you have blamed God for having allowed or even caused. Forgive Him. Release it. Honor, respect and submit to God.

Okay, now return to the beginning of this section, pray through the prayer again and then proceed to the next prayer.

PRAYING GOD'S WORD

Do not seek revenge or bear a grudge against one of your people, but love your neighbor as yourself (Lev. 19:18).

Forgive us our debts, as we also have forgiven our debtors (Matt. 6:12).

For if you forgive men when they sin against you, your heavenly Father will also forgive you. But if you do not forgive men their sins, your Father will not forgive your sins (Matt. 6:14-15).

Then Peter came to Jesus and asked, "Lord, how many times shall I forgive my brother when he sins against me? Up to seven times?" Jesus answered, "I tell you, not seven times, but seventy-seven times" (Matt. 18:21-22).

Be kind and compassionate to one another, forgiving each other, just as in Christ God forgave you (Eph. 4:32).

FLYING FREE FROM THE OCCULT

Lord, I confess that I have sought from Satan the help that should come from God. I confess as sin (name any and all occult sins). I also ask You to forgive me of those sins I cannot remember. In the name of Jesus, I rebuke Satan and his demons and command them to get away from me. I count all things of Satan as my enemies. I close the door on all occult practices, and I command all evil spirits to leave me.

The occult has always been popular, and because of the old sinful nature that resides within everyone, it is becoming more popular all the time. I am writing this from a hotel in Denver, Colorado. This morning before I sat down to write, I grabbed the phone book and looked up "Occult" in the Yellow Pages. There was one listing. I drove there and found a shop full of herbs, horoscopes and other paraphernalia. Much of it looked innocent. The shop offered the kinds of tricks financially unstable people might try in hopes of turning their fortunes. It catered to folks who are going through difficult times and are looking for easy solutions. Mostly, it seemed like fun and games.

But people who dabble in the occult may be unwittingly engaging demonic spirits, and that's why the Bible warns against it so strongly. When we seek from the spiritual world at large the benefits, favors or strength that should only come from God, we are engaging the occult. Deuteronomy 18:10-13 offers plain talk on this subject:

> Let no one be found among you who *sacrifices his son or daughter* in the fire, who practices *divination* or *sorcery*, *interprets omens*, engages in *witchcraft*, or *casts spells*, or who is a *medium* or *spiritist* or who consults the dead. Anyone who does these things is detestable to the LORD, and because of these detestable practices the LORD your God will drive out those nations before you. You must be blameless before the LORD your God (emphasis added).

These verses give us a good overview of the types of things to avoid, some of which seem obvious, but can have subtle meanings:

1. **Sacrificing children**—When we dispose of or neglect our children in order to win spiritual favor (or even to make things more convenient for ourselves), we can open our lives to demonic activity. If you have participated in an abortion, child neglect or abuse, abandoned your children or refused to be responsible for them, you need to repent and renounce those activities and remove the dark root that has formed.

2. **Divination or sorcery**—Diviners are people who try to see into the future or uncover hidden knowledge. Sorcerers are people who engage in black magic—the use of evil powers to create supernatural events. These sound like the kinds of things people don't do anymore, but our culture is still fascinated with diviners and sorcerers. Psychic hotlines, magic tricks, Ouija boards and other means of manipulating the spiritual world and/or controlling others are dangerous—

and the fact that they are commonplace in our culture does not mean they are innocent. Often, people either laugh such things off or play around with them just for fun and then quickly become trapped. It is imperative for us to cleanse our hearts and minds and to confess divination and sorcery as sin before God.

3. **Interpreting omens**—How many times have you been watching a movie where a black cat or crow is used as a sign that bad things are about to happen? People have always been fascinated with omens, or portents, that supposedly hint that bad luck is afoot. Stepping on a crack in a sidewalk? Walking under a ladder? Black cats? Spilling salt? Breaking a mirror? These are all meaningless unless we add faith to them by believing they are bad. We need to confess that such superstition is not merely harmless fun but ungodly. As Christians, we trust God to order every step of our lives.

4. **Engaging in witchcraft**—There is a great deal of discussion today about good witches and bad witches. The bottom line is this: Any spiritual thing that is not either from God's Spirit or from the regenerated human spirit is of darkness. In our culture today, there is a long list of witchcraft activities, both obvious and subtle: new-moon celebrations, the alignment of the planets, horoscopes, channeling, astral projection, fortune-telling, Ouija boards, tarot cards, séances, communication with the dead or any spirit of a human being (dead or alive), mind control, palm reading and voodoo.

5. **Casting spells**—If you have ever done anything to cast a spell on anyone, you have attempted to manipulate demonic spirits. Anytime someone casts a spell, they

end up with demonic activity in their own lives. Whatever they try to place on another impacts them. Confess any attempts to cast spells, and pray for the power of spells over your own life to be broken.

6. **Medium or spiritist**—A medium or spiritist is a person who contacts the spiritual world for others. If someone offers to communicate to the dead for you or tells you they can see into your future using a crystal ball or tea leaves or anything else (other than God's Spirit), run from them as fast as you can. Such folks will open the door of your life to demonic bondage.

7. **Consulting the dead**—When people die, they go into eternity and cannot return to Earth. Generally speaking, if anyone claims to be talking with the dead, they are actually talking with evil spirits who are looking for opportunities to enter the lives of those trying to consult the dead. No doubt, evil spirits will masquerade as the dead person in order to deceive you. But don't be deceived; instead, confess any time you have attended a séance or tried to speak with the dead.

As you can see, the occult is all around us. Examine your life. Is there any area of the occult in which you have dabbled? Are you ready to rely on God and God alone for the grace and wisdom you need to live your life? Repeat the prayer above and then proceed to the next prayer.

PRAYING GOD'S WORD

For the sinful nature desires what is contrary to the Spirit, and the Spirit what is contrary to the sinful nature. They are in conflict with each other, so that you do not do what you want. But if you are led by the Spirit, you are not under law. The acts of the sinful nature are obvious: sexual immorality, impurity and debauchery; idolatry and witchcraft; hatred, discord, jealousy, fits of rage, selfish ambition, dissensions, factions and envy; drunkenness, orgies, and the like. I warn you, as I did before, that those who live like this will not inherit the kingdom of God (Gal. 5:17-21).

Take time to read the accounts in Acts 8 and 19.

FLYING FREE FROM SELF-EXALTATION

Heavenly Father, I come to You in the name of the Lord Jesus Christ. I know arrogance and self-centeredness are abominations to You, and I renounce those sins. I don't want to think more highly of myself than I ought. I humble myself before You and come to You as a little child. Without You, I am conceited and self-centered; but by the power of the Holy Spirit, I can humble myself and become loving and caring toward others.

I ask You to give me blessings that can be used to serve others. Give me favor with people, financial prosperity, innovation and creativity, and the gifts and fruit of the Holy Spirit. Give me wisdom and knowledge. I know that I am nothing without You, but in You I can have the power to live a holy life and make life better for others.

Pride is one of the most deceptive forces the enemy uses to ruin our lives. Proverbs 11:2 says, "When pride comes, then comes disgrace, but with humility comes wisdom." Proverbs 16:18 drives the point home even more strongly: "Pride goes before destruction, a haughty spirit before a fall."

Both of these proverbs reveal the subtle trap pride sets for us. If we let pride or haughtiness develop in our hearts, we are headed for disgrace and destruction. The devil loves to destroy relationships, and pride is one of his most effective tools for weakening our bonds with other people.

Romans 12 is regarded as one of Paul's best explanations of the way believers are supposed to interact with one another. Pastors and teachers quote from it all the time because, in verses 4-8, Paul gives a simple introduction to the idea that different believers have different talents, and these talents work together for the good of the whole Church. But the immediate context of these verses—a discussion of a humble spirit—is often overlooked. Romans 12:3 says, "For by the grace given me I say to every one of you: Do not think of yourself more highly than you ought, but rather think of yourself with sober judgment, in accordance with the measure of faith God has given you." In other words, according to Paul, the only way we can understand how the Body of Christ is supposed to work is by first understanding humility.

Let's back up a little more and look at the two preceding verses:

> Therefore, I urge you, brothers, in view of God's mercy, to offer your bodies as living sacrifices, holy and pleasing to God—this is your spiritual act of worship. Do not conform any longer to the pattern of this world, but be transformed by the renewing of your mind. Then you will be able to test and approve what God's will is—his good, pleasing and perfect will (Rom. 12:1-2).

The world's pattern, as you know, always puts self above others. The world encourages us to believe that it exists for us, that it revolves around us, that people should serve us. We're told to proclaim our opinions and take what is ours. But when we renew our minds with God's Word, we quickly learn that humility is much better—and more powerful—than pride. Humility empowers us and everyone around us to do the work of God, to expand and grow and to achieve like never before.

Humility allows us to discover our proper place, so we can operate in the Body of Christ with great effectiveness. If we don't discover humility, we'll resent people who can't remember our names, speak sharply with coworkers and expect perfect service everywhere we turn. Pride convinces us that we're the most important person of the 6 billion people on Earth, but humility shows us that just the opposite is true: We are here to serve them, to show them unconditional love and grace.

Philippians 2:3-4 urges us, "Do nothing out of selfish ambition or vain conceit, but in humility consider others better than yourselves. Each of you should look not only to your own interests, but also to the interests of others." Paul follows this admonition with an explanation of Jesus' humility—the humble attitude that allowed Him to give Himself up for our sins and suffer for our redemption. With that as our model, how can we be anything but humble before God?

We want to be like Him. Humility is the door through which we must walk. It is the door of personal death, but it leads to life. Pray the prayer above, and then proceed to the next prayer.

℘RAYING GOD'S WORD

[God] mocks proud mockers but gives grace to the humble (Prov. 3:34).

When pride comes, then comes disgrace, but with humility comes wisdom (Prov. 11:2).

Pride goes before destruction, a haughty spirit before a fall (Prov. 16:18).

For everyone who exalts himself will be humbled, and he

who humbles himself will be exalted (Luke 14:11).

For by the grace given me I say to every one of you: Do not think of yourself more highly than you ought, but rather think of yourself with sober judgment, in accordance with the measure of faith God has given you (Rom. 12:3).

Do nothing out of selfish ambition or vain conceit, but in humility consider others better than yourselves. Each of you should look not only to your own interests, but also to the interests of others (Phil. 2:3-4).

Prayer 9

FLYING FREE FROM DARK THOUGHTS

Heavenly Father, in the name of Jesus Christ, the Son of God, I pray that You would cleanse my mind of dark thoughts. I confess that I have let myself be negative, anxious, hateful and sinful in my thinking. I want only to think about things that are true, noble, right, pure, lovely, admirable, excellent and praiseworthy. I want my mind to be filled with peace and life so that I can serve You and bring life to those around me. Lord, renew my mind as I read Your Word and learn to trust in You.

Some of Paul's most stirring words appear in his letter to the Christians in Philippi. He finishes the letter much like you would if you were writing to a good friend that you wanted to exhort. He offers encouragement for all Christians in everyday life—a strong rally call for us to lift up our heads, trust God and refuse to be dominated by dark thoughts about ourselves, anyone or anything. Paul writes:

Rejoice in the Lord always. I will say it again: Rejoice! Let your gentleness be evident to all. The Lord is near. Do not be anxious about anything, but in everything, by prayer and petition, with thanksgiving, present your requests to God. And the peace of God, which transcends all understanding, will guard your hearts and your minds in Christ Jesus. Finally, brothers, whatever is true, whatever is noble, whatever is right, whatever is pure, whatever is lovely, whatever is admirable—if anything is excellent or praiseworthy—think about such things (Phil. 4:4-8).

The condition of our minds is up to us. Our mental habits are up to us. We can decide what to think about, what to dwell on and what mental attitude to have each day. Mental discipline is one of the unique gifts God has given to every one of us. Please understand, I'm not talking about painting on a smile or having optimism—I'm talking about deliberately choosing to trust God, to be filled with the Holy Spirit and to let our minds be disciplined.

This is why communion with God is so important for all of us. Too often we let ourselves be encumbered by the trials of life; or we fill ourselves with ungodly music, books or movies; or we let others' negative attitudes inform our own thoughts; or we let darkness and death sink in through other ways. A life-giving prayer time cleanses us, revives us and sets us free from negative influences.

Often when people are talking with me, they will begin to tell me things about others that I don't need to know. When this happens, I can feel the garbage that has been in them begin to affect me. I don't want to be the garbage can that others can dump into, so I stop them graciously and change the subject, which is one way I discipline my thoughts and attitudes.

I've been suggesting Scriptures for you to pray through in many of these prayer sections, and later in this book you'll read more specifically about praying through the Scriptures. Paul said to "be transformed by the renewing of your mind" (Rom. 12:2), and one of the primary ways mental renewal happens is through reading, learning and meditating on the Word of God. Be sure to read the Bible often, memorize it and let its truths and insights inform your thinking.

By the way, for those of you struggling with mental discipline or learning in general, taking the time to memorize chapters of the Bible and thinking through them when you go to bed will literally transform your mind. I've seen D and F students become A and B students simply by learning portions of Scripture and thinking through them in the evenings. This is spiritually enlightening and helps you practice keeping your mind on track for a period of time. Then, with this discipline, you can apply it to other areas of your life and discover great freedom and opportunity.

Now, pray for freedom from dark thoughts again, and then move on to the next prayer!

PRAYING GOD'S WORD

Whatever is true, whatever is noble, whatever is right, whatever is pure, whatever is lovely, whatever is admirable—if anything is excellent or praiseworthy—think about such things (Phil. 4:8).

Do not conform any longer to the pattern of this world, but be transformed by the renewing of your mind (Rom. 12:2).

Search me, O God, and know my heart; test me and know my anxious thoughts. See if there is any offensive way in me, and lead me in the way everlasting (Ps. 139:23-24).

FLYING FREE FROM DOUBT AND UNBELIEF

Heavenly Father, I confess that I have not had total faith in You. I have doubted Your love and goodness. I have doubted Your presence in my life. I turn from doubt and unbelief and confess my faith and trust in You. I believe that You are the God of heaven and Earth. I believe that You love me. I believe that You have a plan for my life. I place my hope in You, Lord, and I am confident in Your truth.

There is a difference between questioning Christian ideas and doubting God. Often people become unnecessarily guilty as they question various interpretations of Scripture or learn to distinguish good doctrine from false doctrine. You will always be learning and growing, and if you become confused about the wonderfully mysterious issues of faith from time to time, there is no reason to worry.

But it is vital that we trust God in the midst of the process. Particularly in times of crisis in our lives, we cannot be stubborn in our thinking or refuse to live in love and truth. Willful doubt and unbelief is sinful—it is our responsibility to trust Him, to believe in Him, to let Him guide us even when things seem unclear.

How do we know whether or not we are trusting God? One litmus test the Bible offers is love and obedience. First John 3:18-24 says:

> Dear children, let us love not with words or tongue but with actions and in truth. This then is how we know that we belong to the truth, and how we set our hearts at rest in his presence whenever our hearts condemn us. For God is greater than our hearts, and he knows everything. Dear friends, if our hearts do not condemn us, we have confidence before God and receive from him anything we ask, because we obey his commands and do what pleases him. And this is his command: to believe in the name of his Son, Jesus Christ, and to love one another as he commanded us. Those who obey his commands live in him, and he in them. And this is how we know that he lives in us: We know it by the Spirit he gave us.

The Bible is filled with fantastic, smart explanations of faith like this one. If you're struggling with doubt and unbelief, grab a Bible with a concordance; look up the words "faith," "faithful," "faithfulness," etc.; and read every Scripture you can. There are hundreds of passages on faith. As you read through them, pray through them and confess your doubts and receive His love, forgiveness and wisdom, you will grow in God's truth with amazing power and insight.

Romans 10:17 says, "Consequently, faith comes from hearing the message, and the message is heard through the word of Christ." Because of this, I have committed to read at least a small portion of the Bible every day. Why? Because I receive faith when I read the Bible. Meditate on the following verses. Then pray the prayer above again as you commit to faith in Christ.

PRAYING GOD'S WORD

For the LORD gives wisdom, and from his mouth come knowledge and understanding (Prov. 2:6).

Jesus answered, "The work of God is this: to believe in the one he has sent" (John 6:29).

Where is the wise man? Where is the scholar? Where is the philosopher of this age? Has not God made foolish the wisdom of the world? For since in the wisdom of God the world through its wisdom did not know him, God was pleased through the foolishness of what was preached to save those who believe. Jews demand miraculous signs and Greeks look for wisdom, but we preach Christ crucified: a stumbling block to Jews and foolishness to Gentiles, but to those whom God has called, both Jews and Greeks, Christ the power of God and the wisdom of God. For the foolishness of God is wiser than man's wisdom, and the weakness of God is stronger than man's strength (1 Cor. 1:20-25).

FLYING FREE FROM NEGATIVE SPIRITUAL AND EMOTIONAL TIES

In the name of Jesus, I break every negative spiritual and emotional tie in my life. I pray that You, Lord, would free me of the sins of my past. I confess that I have had negative relationships with (name them), and I pray that You would break the spiritual power of those relationships and set me free so that my heart can be innocent, clean and free to serve You.

When King David was a young man, he developed a very close relationship with another man named Jonathan. The two were best friends who were willing to do anything for one another. The Bible says that "Jonathan became one in spirit with David, and he loved him as himself" (1 Sam. 18:1). The *King James Version* puts it this way: "The soul of Jonathan was knit with the soul of David, and Jonathan loved him as his own soul." So when people develop particularly close relationships, we often refer to those relationships as soul ties. Those ties can be either positive or negative, depending on the nature of the relationships. Positive soul ties are among the best blessings

in life, but negative soul ties can have devastating consequences if they are not broken. Sometimes people with severe
emotional disturbances are tied to relationships that began
several years earlier.

What kinds of relationships develop negative soul ties?
Anytime we get abnormally close with someone we shouldn't,
become overly attached to someone we shouldn't or develop a
sexual relationship outside of marriage, we are developing a negative soul tie. Those ties can affect other areas of our lives for
years if we don't deal with them in prayer and break their power
over our lives.

Negative soul ties form between people if they establish a
blood covenant with one another. Very often, people have
formed negative soul ties by masturbating while looking at
pornographic magazines, videos or Internet sites. The Bible says
that we become one with those we have sexual relations with,
and Jesus warned us that to lust in our hearts is the same as actually committing the act. This is a grave situation for those who
have a history of immorality and are trying to find freedom.
Thankfully, though, all it takes is a prayer to sever these ties
because the name of Jesus is so strong.

Just as positive spiritual and emotional ties strengthen us to
do well in life, so negative spiritual and emotional ties grip our
hearts and tug us toward darkness.

God wants us to love everyone in a wholesome, honorable
way. And there will be a few people in our lives to whom we are
unusually close: family, friends, some coworkers and colaborers
for the gospel. For those relationships to be strong and healthy,
our hearts need to be clean and full of life. The residue of old,
damaging relationships needs to be wiped clean through the
blood of Jesus and the power of the Holy Spirit. Pray the above
prayer again. This time ask God to bring to your memory any
old relationships you may need to address.

PRAYING GOD'S WORD

Be very careful, then, how you live—not as unwise but as wise, making the most of every opportunity, because the days are evil (Eph. 5:15-16).

May God himself, the God of peace, sanctify you through and through. May your whole spirit, soul and body be kept blameless at the coming of our Lord Jesus Christ. The one who calls you is faithful and he will do it (1 Thess. 5:23-24).

FLYING FREE FROM OCCULT BONDAGE AND THE EFFECTS OF NEGATIVE WORDS

Heavenly Father, in the name of the Lord Jesus Christ, I now rebuke, break and loose myself and my children from any and all evil curses, charms, vexes, hexes, spells, jinxes, psychic powers, bewitchment, witchcraft and sorcery that may have been put upon me or my family from any people or from any occult or psychic sources; and I cancel all connected and related spirits and command them to leave me. I break the power of any negative word that has ever been spoken against me or anyone in my family. I thank You, Lord, for setting me free.

Theologians, sociologists, politicians, psychologists and philosophers have debated for centuries about the effects of words. As you know, we sometimes pay a significant amount of money to have people talk to us. And all of us have seen crowds transform their opinions and actions because of words.

Obviously God cares about words since He reveals Himself through the written Word, the Bible, and demonstrates Himself through the living Word, Jesus Himself.

Without a doubt, words impact our thoughts, but no one is sure about the spiritual impact words have on people. We know that harsh, thoughtless words from an adult toward a child can certainly crush their spirits and damage them deeply. We also know that the book of James emphasizes the importance of our speech in order to live a godly life. James 3:9 says, "With the tongue we praise our Lord and Father, and with it we curse men, who have been made in God's likeness."

When we praise God, pray, repent or petition God, we know that our words touch the heart of God and stimulate the Holy Spirit's activity around us. When we pray for others, the Holy Spirit's work increases around them. And when the Holy Spirit's work intensifies in another's life because of our prayers, we know that as a consequence the influence of the world and darkness decreases.

The same is true with negative words. When we say negative things about ourselves, our families, our churches and our community, we might just be saying empty words. But then again we may be activating dark, negative spiritual activity around those about whom we are saying negative things. Proverbs 18:21 (*KJV*) says, "Death and life are in the power of the tongue." In other words, when we bless others, those words have an impact. When negative things are said, sometimes there is a spiritual response to those words and demonic spirits try to fulfill the negative words. Just as blessings are able to activate the power of God, so curses activate the power of darkness.

I pray a prayer similar to the one above every week over the church I pastor. Why? Because I know that people casually say negative things about the Body of Christ and might say something negative about some of the families in the church, my family or me. Then, of course, there are those who are involved in satanism or witchcraft and that involvement could be actively releasing negative power to discourage believers or the Body of Christ at large. This simple prayer negates those efforts. It's terrific when we use the power God has given us to ensure that darkness never gains a foothold among God's people.

PRAYING GOD'S WORD

Death and life are in the power of the tongue: and they that love it shall eat the fruit thereof (Prov. 18:21, *KJV*).

He who guards his mouth and his tongue keeps himself from calamity (Prov. 21:23).

Do not let any unwholesome talk come out of your mouths, but only what is helpful for building others up according to their needs, that it may benefit those who listen (Eph. 4:29).

The tongue is a small part of the body, but it makes great boasts. Consider what a great forest is set on fire by a small spark. The tongue also is a fire, a world of evil among the parts of the body. It corrupts the whole person, sets the whole course of his life on fire, and is itself set on fire by hell (Jas. 3:5-6).

Prayer 13

FLYING FREE FROM INTERNAL DIVISION

Heavenly Father, I want to be whole. I want to be complete in You. I confess that I have been double-minded in some areas of my life, and because of this I have not had my feet firmly planted. I set my mind, will and emotions 100 percent toward the service of the Lord Jesus Christ. I am determined to be confident in You and Your purposes for my life. I trust you, and I pray that everything within me will focus on Your perfect plan. I receive Your will to rule my life. Clear my mind and focus me on Your will for me. I set my eyes on You now, and I thank You for making me stable, strong and confident.

The Bible is filled with strong exhortations like this for us to be focused and secure in our knowledge of God and His will for our lives. In the Old Testament, we read about the great men of faith such as Abraham, Jacob, Isaac, Joseph, Moses, David, Job and many more. Why were those men great? Because they were not internally divided. They trusted God. They let Him point them in a direction, and they stayed on the path He provided for them.

Jesus spoke about this in strong language: "No one who puts his hand to the plow and looks back is fit for service in the kingdom of God" (Luke 9:62). God wants us to remain focused no matter what happens. Peter, Paul and the apostles faced phenomenally difficult trials (you can read about them in Acts—it's exciting stuff!), and they refused to budge from their conviction that Jesus is Lord.

How can we avoid being internally divided? Well, you are doing it right now. By reading this book, growing in your prayer life and praying through the Scriptures, you are renewing your mind and becoming whole, single-minded and determined. If you stay committed to prayer, Bible study and a healthy church life, your mind will be free and clear. You won't be divided, trying to go in two different directions at the same time. You will know how to serve God. Go for it!

Psalm 23:3 records this declaration by King David: "[God] restores my soul." What does this mean? Well, it means that David is grateful for God taking his life and causing his entire being to be focused in one direction. His mind, will and emotions all work together to create in him God's perfect will. Sin fragments our souls, and we find ourselves pulling against ourselves as we navigate through life. People with a fragmented soul are double-minded, undisciplined and very often unable to make or keep commitments. In this prayer, we are asking God to undo the fragmenting effects of disobedience in our lives and to align us, bringing integrity to dominate every area of our lives.

_PRAYING GOD'S WORD

Do not turn aside from any of the commands I give you today, to the right or to the left, following other gods and serving them (Deut. 28:14).

Be strong and very courageous. Be careful to obey all the law my servant Moses gave you; do not turn from it to the right or to the left, that you may be successful wherever you go (Josh. 1:7).

Let your eyes look straight ahead, fix your gaze directly before you. Make level paths for your feet and take only ways that are firm. Do not swerve to the right or the left; keep your foot from evil (Prov. 4:25-27).

Like a city whose walls are broken down is a man who lacks self-control (Prov. 25:28).

SOARING WITH FREEDOM

Heavenly Father, I thank You that You have made me free to soar in You. Thank You for freeing me from my sins. Thank You for giving me eternal life. Thank You for baptizing me in Your Spirit. I love growing in Your presence. I am so thankful that You have released me from the powers of darkness and evil and that You have made me whole, complete, innocent and clean in Your sight. I love You and I want to serve You more. I pray that You would cause me to soar in Your gifts and in the power of the Holy Spirit. I eagerly desire to grow in love and peace. I want to prophesy, intercede, speak in tongues, heal sickness, have incredible faith and do anything else that will serve others and please You. I want to be used by You, Lord. Thank You for loving me. Thank You for giving me life. I am so happy that You have rescued me from sin and death and are filling me with life every day. Do whatever You want to do in me, God! I am Yours.

Congratulations! You have learned over a dozen vital life-giving prayers. You know how to pray for salvation, how to be baptized in the Holy Spirit and how to pray for healing and freedom from demonic activity. You know how to be liberated from judgment, the occult, dark thoughts, doubt and unbelief and other negative influences. In the rest of this book, I want to introduce you to some other key prayers that can really establish your life on God's Word and the power of the Holy Spirit. You have built a solid foundation at this point, and you can keep building it and making it stronger as you work through these prayers over and over again.

Continue to enjoy your prayer times. Set them apart as holy times to commune with God. He loves that you are praying to Him, and He enjoys the time you spend seeking His presence and growing in His gifts of love and freedom. He wants to give you more and more.

PRAYING GOD'S WORD

And when you pray, do not be like the hypocrites, for they love to pray standing in the synagogues and on the street corners to be seen by men. I tell you the truth, they have received their reward in full. But when you pray, go into your room, close the door and pray to your Father, who is unseen. Then your Father, who sees what is done in secret, will reward you. And when you pray, do not keep on babbling like pagans, for they think they will be heard because of their many words. Do not be like them, for your Father knows what you need before you ask him (Matt. 6:5-8).

Be joyful always; pray continually; give thanks in all circumstances, for this is God's will for you in Christ Jesus (1 Thess. 5:16-18).

SOARING
PRAYERS

Living Daily by the Power
of the Holy Spirit

Prayer 15

SOARING THROUGH THE DOOR OF THE CROSS

Jesus, I thank You for Your work on the Cross. I thank You that You took my sins upon Yourself and made me new. I thank You that, because of Your resurrection, I have new life. Father, I count myself crucified with Christ. I kill the old sinful nature and all of its fleshly desires. I renounce pride and selfishness and my own needs and wants. I ask You to fill me with the life of God. Holy Spirit, I ask You to come and manifest Your life in me. Let me live as You live. I want to say what You're saying and go where You're going and do what You're doing. O God, come and be alive in me!

Sometimes people ask me how I can keep going, day after day, serving God with faithfulness and strength. I love to look them in the eye and say, "It's easy: I kill myself every day." After they recover from their initial shock, I calm their fears by explaining what I mean. The only way to grow strong in the Lord and to continue serving Him is to crucify the old sinful nature every day—dying to yourself and your desires and living every moment as unto God.

I will never forget listening to Dr. Cho, the pastor of the world's largest church in Seoul, Korea, telling a conference of thousands of pastors how much he struggles with hating people. Cho confessed that as he works with people from week to week, he sometimes finds himself dealing with resentment toward others—even his own church elders! When the nervous laughter subsided, he made this profoundly powerful statement: "I don't pray because I'm good; I pray because I'm so evil."

That is true for all of us. Too often we try to find noble reasons within ourselves for drawing near to God. We pretend that we meet with God because we are good enough or, more likely, we avoid praying because we don't feel righteous enough. Yet the primary reason to draw near to God is because we need Him. Hebrews 4:16 encourages us: "Let us then approach the throne of grace with confidence, so that we may receive mercy and find grace to help us in time of need."

In giving us Himself, God has given us everything that we need. The way to appropriate that power is to open ourselves up to Him every day by crucifying the old sinful nature and allowing the life of God to flow strong in us. The apostle Paul knew this principle well. He understood that the old sinful nature and the Holy Spirit are in conflict with each other. In his letter to the Galatians, Paul lists the works of the flesh as "sexual immorality, impurity and debauchery; idolatry and witchcraft; hatred, discord, jealousy, fits of rage, selfish ambition, dissensions, factions and envy; drunkenness, orgies, and the like" (5:19-21).

Whether we realize it or not, all of us have the potential for such horrible evil because we all have an old sinful nature. Without Christ, we are doomed to follow those impulses, leading to destruction. But thank God for Jesus Christ! Because of His death and resurrection, we have the Holy Spirit living inside us. The fruit that the Spirit of God produces is "love, joy, peace, patience, kindness, goodness, faithfulness, gentleness and self-control" (Gal. 5:22-23). Paul makes it very clear that the way to avoid giving in to the desires of our flesh is to "live by the Spirit" (Gal. 5:25). Paul gives us a clue into how we can live by the Spirit every day when he describes his own life. "I have been crucified with Christ," he writes, "and I no longer live, but Christ lives in me. The life I live in the body, I live by faith in the Son of God, who loved me and gave himself for me" (Gal. 2:20).

It is tempting to make our spiritual growth a matter of our own determination. We can easily fall into the trap of working as if everything depends on us. The truth is, without the life of God flowing in us and through us, we are absolutely helpless. So, you see, we pray because we need God. We need His life and His nature to be made manifest in us through the Holy Spirit. The road to life goes through the door of the Cross.

Return again to the prayer at the beginning of this chapter. Make the decision to "die daily." Ask God to flood your heart with His life, His love and all the fruit of the Spirit. Then, with open hands and an open heart, allow Him to do it.

PRAYING GOD'S WORD

You, however, are controlled not by the sinful nature but by the Spirit, if the Spirit of God lives in you. And if anyone does not have the Spirit of Christ, he does not belong to Christ. But if Christ is in you, your body is dead because of sin, yet your spirit is alive because of righteousness (Rom. 8:9-10).

Therefore, I urge you, brothers, in view of God's mercy, to offer your bodies as living sacrifices, holy and pleasing to God—this is your spiritual act of worship. Do not conform any longer to the pattern of this world, but be transformed by the renewing of your mind. Then you will be able to test and approve what God's will is—his good, pleasing and perfect will (Rom. 12:1-2).

I have been crucified with Christ and I no longer live, but Christ lives in me. The life I live in the body, I live by faith in the Son of God, who loved me and gave himself for me (Gal. 2:20).

Let us then approach the throne of grace with confidence, so that we may receive mercy and find grace to help us in time of need (Heb. 4:16).

Prayer 16

SOARING THROUGH PRAYING THE SCRIPTURES

Heavenly Father, I submit my life to the Word of God, the Bible. I believe that there is power in Your Word. I recognize that it is eternal, unchanging and perfect. I acknowledge that the Bible is alive and active, has power to defeat demonic schemes and shines light into the darkness. I need Your power to live a successful life in Christ, so I claim the promises that You make in the Bible. As I pray about the ideas from Your Word, I ask You to release the gift of faith in me.

Just like David prayed so long ago, so now I say to You that as "the deer pants for streams of water, so my soul pants for you, O God" (Ps. 42:1). I want to know You the way that David knew You. Cause my heart to burn continually for You.

In accordance with Your Word, Father, I refuse to worry about anything. I trust that You know my needs, and I choose today to seek first Your kingdom and Your righteousness in my life. I believe that all the things I need will be given to me as well (see Matt. 6:32-33). Help me to trust in Your provision and seek You in everything I do.

And Lord, let love, joy, peace, patience, kindness, goodness, faithfulness, gentleness and self-control flow out of my life today by the power of the Holy Spirit (see Gal. 5:22-23). Let me be a blessing to the people I encounter today, and cause them to see something of Your character in me. Thank You, Father, for the power of Your Word. Help me to sow it into my life.

The great thing about this prayer is that it is endless. These are two examples of Scriptures that I pray into my life every day, but there are thousands more. God's Word regarding worship, warfare, brokenness, power—everything I've been discussing in the course of this book is all in the Scriptures.

We need to remember the immeasurable wealth to be found in the Bible, especially when we want to pray but have difficulty finding the words to say. "Jesus asked us to tarry an hour with him," a man from our church said as he sank into the chair in my office. "But I've prayed for my family, confessed my sins, thanked God for my home, my job and my church. I've prayed everything I can think of, and I still have 58 minutes to go!" Too often this kind of discouragement leads to a dead prayer life. A powerful way to energize your prayer life is simply to pray back to God the promises and exhortations He makes to you in the Bible.

All that's involved in praying the Scriptures is reading or reciting a verse or passage, expounding on the main ideas and then applying them to your life. So if you are entering a time of repentance, you might flip to Psalm 51:1 and read to the Lord, "Have mercy on me, O God, according to your unfailing love; according to your great compassion blot out my transgressions." Your prayer might then continue, "O Father, I praise you for your great love and mercy. Thank you for being willing to blot out my sins." And then the next verse: "Wash away all my iniquity and cleanse me from my sin," followed by your prayer, "Please forgive my sins, O God . . ."

As we pray the ideas of the Scriptures, we sow their power into our lives. The Bible tells us that the Word of God "is living and active. Sharper than any double-edged sword, it penetrates even to dividing soul and spirit, joints and marrow; it judges the thoughts and attitudes of the heart" (Heb. 4:12). When we sow the Scriptures into our hearts, we will reap the power to change our attitudes, break sinful patterns in our lives and be filled with God's love for the lost. Why pray with our words alone when there is so much life-changing power in His Word?

Two important, life-changing purposes of biblical prayer are communing with God and confronting demonic schemes. Praying the Scriptures is certainly valuable in connecting with God. Because God spoke His ideas into the heart of the Bible authors, and then those ideas were translated into the language you speak, you can get a glimpse of God—His heart, His thoughts, His purpose and plan for your life.

But praying Scripture is also essential when we engage in spiritual warfare prayer. In Matthew 4, Jesus is led by the Holy Spirit into the wilderness to be tempted by the devil. In the ultimate bout of spiritual warfare, Jesus combats the evil one with just one weapon—the powerful Word of the Father. Weary, lonesome and famished after 40 days of fasting, Jesus could have been in a precarious position against His cunning adversary. Instead of relying on His natural strength and intellect, the Lord Jesus responds to each wave of the devil's attack with Scripture: "*It is written* . . ." (Matt. 4:4, emphasis added). He unsheathes the powerful sword of the Spirit, and the devil doesn't stand a chance. Likewise, when we engage in warfare prayer with our own weapons, we are powerless, fighting with the weapons of the flesh. But armed with the Word of God, we have great power to combat the ancient foe.

So as you seek after God's heart, put to death the sinful nature and dismantle the plans of the enemy, tap into the power of the Word of God and give your prayer times a fresh charge of power. When we pray the ideas from the Word of God, He again breathes into our hearts and illuminates the Word of God in our minds and our spirits. We do more than believe the Bible; in addition, God, by His Spirit, infuses the ideas of the Bible into our hearts, so we are actually transformed on the inside to conform to the principles of the Bible. Thus, the Bible actually sanctifies us from the inside out when we pray the Scriptures. Have fun!

*P*RAYING GOD'S WORD

The word of God is living and active. Sharper than any double-edged sword, it penetrates even to dividing soul and spirit, joints and marrow; it judges the thoughts and attitudes of the heart (Heb. 4:12).

The weapons we fight with are not the weapons of the world. On the contrary, they have divine power to demolish strongholds (2 Cor. 10:4).

All Scripture is God-breathed and is useful for teaching, rebuking, correcting and training in righteousness, so that the man of God may be thoroughly equipped for every good work (2 Tim. 3:16-17).

Do not be anxious about anything (Phil. 4:6).

Stand firm. Let nothing move you. Always give yourself fully to the work of the Lord (1 Cor. 15:58).

Praise the Lord, O my soul; all my inmost being, praise his holy name (Ps. 103:1).

SOARING THROUGH PRAYING FOR AUTHORITIES

Heavenly Father, I pray for all those who are in authority over me. I thank You for those in my family who have authority over me, and I pray that You would protect them and give them wisdom. I also pray for those in authority over me at work, and I ask You to give them innovative ideas so that our business will prosper. Thank You for our country, Lord. I pray for those who have authority over me in our country and, Lord, I pray for our church leadership, that You would bless them and keep them in Your hand.

Lord, I submit myself to their authority out of reverence to You. I recognize that You have placed them in authority over me. I choose to forgive them for their failures and shortcomings. Keep me from resentment and bitterness. Help me always to support and obey them as I submit to You. I ask that Your kingdom come and Your will be done through them, in me and in the spheres of influence You have given them.

God has delegated His authority to four structures on Earth: family, workplace, government and church. He promises in

1 Timothy 2:2 that if we pray for those in authority over us, then we will live "peaceful and quiet lives in all godliness and holiness." Then He highlights this idea by saying that such prayer is good, and pleasing to Him, for our Lord wants all to be saved and to come to a knowledge of the truth (see 2 Tim. 2:3).

The ramifications of this Scripture are huge if we regularly pray for those in authority over us:

1. Authority will not be abused and misused as we so commonly see it today.
2. We will be able to live in great peace.
3. We will be able to enjoy a quiet life without shame, hurt, anger, and bitterness.
4. We will be able to live a godly life with much greater ease.
5. We will be able to live a holy life with much greater ease.

What a set of promises! But that's not all. Then the Scripture tells us that praying for those in authority over us has a direct bearing on evangelism. How? Because when believers pray for those in authority, it causes their families, businesses, governments and churches to enjoy greater blessing from God and freedom from darkness and the world.

This is why Paul writes to the Romans, "[The one in authority] is God's servant to do you good. But if you do wrong, be afraid. . . . He is God's servant, an agent of wrath to bring punishment on the wrongdoer" (Rom. 13:4). Authorities are in place to make life better for all of us, which is why Paul says, "Everyone must submit himself to the governing authorities, for there is no authority except that which God has established. The authorities that exist have been established by God" (Rom. 13:1).

But what do we do when authorities are corrupt? Well, it depends on the nature of the corruption, and certainly God has raised up people throughout history to overthrow evil authorities.

But I maintain that we are to respect and submit to our authorities. One of the greatest tests of our character is how we deal with weaknesses in the lives of others, and we have a choice as to how we respond to the failures of those in authority over us. We can get bitter and cynical, or we can honor them as God's authority over us. I'm not talking about hiding their sin—I'm talking about keeping a clean heart.

One of the best ways to keep our hearts pure and submitted to the authorities that God has placed in our lives is to pray for them every day. Pray that God would be gracious to them, that His mercy would cover them. Praying this helps us to release them from their failures and to forgive them. As we pray and ask God's blessing over them, we are acknowledging that He has placed them there. Furthermore, by praying for those in authority over us, we invite God to do His will through them. On a personal level, we are opening ourselves to receive blessings from God through those in authority, whether it is correction, guidance or encouragement. But on a larger scale, when we as Christians full of the Holy Spirit pray for those in authority, we are bringing the influence of the kingdom of God to our families, workplaces, cities, nations and churches.

I have a list of the four authority structures and the names of those in authority over me, so I can pray for them. I'll share my simple outline with you, but it's up to you to fill in the blanks!

Family—List parents, grandparents, and/or guardians that are still living. In addition, pray for older brothers and sisters.

Workplace—List those above you in the chain of command of the business. If you own the company, pray for your customers. You work for them.

Government—List the president, vice president and their cabinet members. In addition, list your two senators and your congressperson, and list the nine Supreme Court justices. Do the same thing with your state, which means you list the names of your governor, lieutenant governor and the governor's cabinet. List the members of the state senate and your local representative, as well as the judges who sit on the state supreme court. You can do the same type of lists for your county and your city.

Church—I have a list of global Christian leaders, national Christian leaders and the leadership team of our local church.

Once you make this list, insert it into this book at this spot or keep it in some other handy place, so you can refer to it when you pray. You'll find wonderful joy in praying for those who have authority over you, and you'll find great delight as you see your prayers answered. Remember, prayer stimulates the Holy Spirit's activity.

PRAYING GOD'S WORD

Everyone must submit himself to the governing authorities, for there is no authority except that which God has established. The authorities that exist have been established by God (Rom. 13:1).

I urge, then, first of all, that requests, prayers, intercession and thanksgiving be made for everyone—for kings and all those in authority, that we may live peaceful and quiet lives in all godliness and holiness (1 Tim. 2:1-2).

Prayer 18

SOARING THROUGH PROPHETIC INTERCESSION

Heavenly Father, Your Word says that we should "eagerly desire spiritual gifts, especially the gift of prophecy" (1 Cor. 14:1). Sometimes, Father, I feel like I am too random when I pray. I want to know You, and I want my intercession to flow with what the Holy Spirit is doing, so I need to hear from You clearly. Speak to me, Lord, and make my prayers targeted and strategic. I know that the time is growing short and the days are evil, and I want to make the most of my time here on Earth. So Father, tune my heart to hear Your voice with crystal clarity as I pray. Quiet the competing influences of my flesh and the enemy, and help me to be attentive to Your Spirit. Direct my intercession in order to make the greatest impact for the kingdom of God as it forcefully advances here on Earth.

Lord, please accomplish Your work through me as I pray. Give me insight in order to thwart the devil's schemes in my life and others' lives and to pray for the people that are on Your heart. I love serving You, God, and I love hearing Your voice. Speak to me now.

Prophetic intercession is simply hearing the voice of God with clarity and responding in your prayers. It is, in effect, formalizing the two-way nature of communication with God. When we pray prophetically, we are opening our spiritual ears to hear God's specific directions and then targeting those areas in our prayers.

Typically, prophetic insight is not something that happens instantly—it takes cultivating, like a vegetable garden or a new relationship. But 1 Corinthians 14 is clear about the availability and desirability of the gift of prophecy, so seek and ye shall find!

Why is it important for us to hear the voice of God and intercede accordingly in our prayer times? There are two reasons. First, the devil is real, and he is no joke. The Bible says, "Be self-controlled and alert. Your enemy the devil prowls around like a roaring lion looking for someone to devour" (1 Pet. 5:8). The true and right notion that we are victorious over the enemy is too often distorted into the notion that the devil is a pushover. But he is no pansy. He was defeated on the Cross, but his power is still real, and his plans to destroy people's lives are real. Though the devil's victories are always temporary, Paul calls him "the god of this age" (2 Cor. 4:4) and refers to his upper management as "the rulers, . . . the authorities, . . . the powers of this dark world" (Eph. 6:12). We do have the assurance of knowing the end of the story, but for now, we must grapple with this formidable foe using the weapons that are available to us.

In his book on strategic-level spiritual warfare entitled *Confronting the Powers*, Dr. Peter Wagner refers to the advent of a set of new "spiritual technology" that we must harness and employ against the enemy. Among this spiritual technology, he asserts, is prophetic intercession. Because the enemy is real, active, and powerful, it is essential that we be informed of his targets and strategies.[1] In a real sense, the Holy Spirit is our reconnaissance squad—our scout snooping out across enemy lines and reporting back intelligence, so we'll know how to attack in prayer.

The second reason prophetic intercession is important to our faith journey is that we simply need help in our prayers. Romans 8:26 says, "The Spirit helps us in our weakness. We do not know what we ought to pray for, but the Spirit himself intercedes for us." When we listen for the voice of the God, He guides and directs us in our prayers in order to make them more effective. The Holy Spirit functions like the scope on a rifle. Can you hit your target by eyeballing it? Sure, maybe—I don't know. But when the hunter hones in on his target, his accuracy increases exponentially. Likewise, when our prayers are focused by the prophetic unction of the Holy Spirit, their effectiveness magnifies.

Before you pray through the prayer at the beginning of this chapter again, read 1 Corinthians 14. Ask God to work the gift of prophecy into your life, and determine to keep asking Him this in your daily prayer time until you begin to hear His voice with clarity. Then pray through the prayer as a launching pad into prophetic intercession. And remember, it takes cultivating, so practice hearing the voice of God and responding in your times of prayer.

PRAYING GOD'S WORD

Follow the way of love and eagerly desire spiritual gifts, especially the gift of prophecy. For anyone who speaks in a tongue does not speak to men but to God. Indeed, no one understands him; he utters mysteries with his spirit. He who prophesies edifies the church (1 Cor. 14:1-2,4).

Note
1. C. Peter Wagner, *Confronting the Powers* (Ventura, CA: Regal Books, 1996), pp. 30, 91, 96.

SOARING THROUGH LOVE

Heavenly Father, I thank You for Your great love for me. I thank You that because of Your love, You came and rescued me. Even while I was still in sin, still an enemy of God, You gave Your life to make me Your friend. I want a deeper understanding of Your love for me. Let Your love come alive in my heart. Cause me to love You like I never have before. Captivate my heart with Your love!

Lord, please help me to see people as You see them and to love them as You love me. Put Your love inside me, so the world can see You through me. I love You, God!

I love people! I am so thankful for the relationships that I have. I love my wife, I love my children, and I love my friends. Sometimes I am just bursting with joy because of all the wonderful people God has placed in my life. It is a beautiful thing to be full of love for those who surround you day in and day out. I am convinced that human beings were made to be in loving relationships with each other. You know why? Because we are made in the image of God, and God is a highly relational being.

The Bible says it simply: "God is love" (1 John 4:16). What does that mean? Well, it means that not only is He consumed with love for us, but also He exists in a mysterious love relationship within Himself. We call it the Trinity. God is three Persons in one being: Father, Son, Holy Spirit—a mysterious union of three distinct personalities in constant communion with each other. This union is loving and relational, and since God made humans in the likeness of His image (see Gen. 1:27), we love other people and want to be in relationship with them.

But there is a problem. All of our human loves—the love shared by a family, the love in friendships and the love that draws together husband and wife—as glorious and noble as they appear, are flawed. Our fallen nature can easily pervert these loves, resulting in twisted relationships that hurt, instead of heal. If we follow our misguided notions of love, we can find ourselves quickly hurtling down a path of self-destruction, sometimes dragging others along as well. We need the love of God to make our human loves work.

That is why it is so important to have a deep understanding of God's love for us. The apostle Paul, writing to the Ephesians, prays that they, "being rooted and established in love, may have power, together with all the saints, to grasp how wide and long and high and deep is the love of Christ, and to know this love that surpasses knowledge" (Eph. 3:17-19). You see, it is God's love that defines for us what love is. The apostle John writes, "This is how we know what love is: Jesus Christ laid down his life for us" (1 John 3:16). God defines love. That is why a proper understanding of God's love for us is the cornerstone of all healthy relationships.

Think about our relationship with God: "We love because he first loved us" (1 John 4:19). He is the one who initiated a relationship with us. We don't love God because we have such noble hearts. No! We love God because He gave us life; He found us lost in our sin, came down from heaven in the form of mortal man and gave His life to save us. The apostle John writes, "This is love: not that we loved God, but that he loved us and sent his Son as an atoning sacrifice for our sins" (1 John 4:10). When we see how great and marvelous the love of God for us is, we cannot help but love Him. Our love for God increases in direct proportion to our understanding of His love for us.

Jesus told His disciples that He loved them as the Father loved Him. Do you see the pattern? The Father loves the Son because God is love; the Son loves us as the Father loves Him; we love each other as Jesus loves us; and as a result, people will love God because they see His love for them in us. The circle is complete. So let the love of God fill your heart. Let Him draw you to Himself. Ask Him to help you see people as He sees them. By allowing the love of God to flow in your life, you are an ambassador of His love to the world, drawing their hearts to love Him, too.

PRAYING GOD'S WORD

For God so loved the world that he gave his one and only Son, that whoever believes in him shall not perish but have eternal life (John 3:16).

As the Father has loved me, so have I loved you. Now remain in my love. If you obey my commands, you will remain in my love, just as I have obeyed my Father's commands and remain in his love. I have told you this so that my joy may be in you and that your joy may be complete. My command is this: Love each other as I have loved you. Greater love has no one than this, that he lay down his life for his friends (John 15:9-13).

Dear friends, let us love one another, for love comes from God. Everyone who loves has been born of God and knows God. Whoever does not love does not know God, because God is love. This is how God showed his love among us: He sent his one and only Son into the world that we might live through him. This is love: not that we loved God, but that he loved us and sent his Son as an atoning sacrifice for our sins. Dear friends, since God so loved us, we also ought to love one another. No one has ever seen God; but if we love one another, God lives in us and his love is made complete in us (1 John 4:7-12).

SOARING THROUGH JUSTICE

Heavenly Father, You are a good God, full of love and compassion. Thank You for sending Your Spirit into my heart, so I can be Your instrument to show Your love and compassion for people. As I spend my life serving You and loving people, I thank You that You have given me resources, influence, wisdom, compassion and the internal strength necessary to help others. Prosper me, so I can be generous on every occasion; and open my eyes, so I can clearly see the horror of poverty, injustice and repression that is so rampant in the world. Cause my heart to beat after Your own as I consider the sacrifice You made for every person. Give me the grace, O God, to see others as You do— precious and valuable—and to work as Your servant to assist those who cannot help themselves.

Lord, I pray for the poor, the deprived and the mistreated. Have mercy on them and save them from peril. Use all of us who love Your name to be their defender and champion, mighty God. Assign angels to stand with us as we war against injustice in the world, and strengthen our hearts by Your Spirit as we work to stamp out oppression. Your Word says that the one whom the Son has set free is free indeed. In Your power I ask that You would use me to set people free.

The United States' Declaration of Independence trumpets a fundamental truth that the Scriptures establish: *All people are created equal.* The Old Testament points out our lives' infinitesimal brevity compared with God's (see Ps. 39) and establishes the sinful nature of every person (see Pss. 14, 53). In that sense, we are all the same. The prophet Micah implores God's people to act accordingly: "He has showed you, O man, what is good. And what does the LORD require of you? To act justly and to love mercy and to walk humbly with your God" (Micah 6:8). The *King James Version* highlights the point, translating the phrase as "to do justly." God judges justly, and He expects you and me to do the same.

In the New Testament, the apostle Paul affirms God's conviction that we are all equally valuable: "You are all sons of God through faith in Christ Jesus. . . . There is neither Jew nor Greek, slave nor free, male nor female, for you are all one in Christ Jesus. If you belong to Christ, then you are Abraham's seed, and heirs according to the promise" (Gal. 3:26-29).

Across our country and throughout the world, one people, race, class or sex are committing all manner of atrocities against another because they do not know or do not believe in the inherent equality and humanity of all people. Men have forced women into brutal and degrading subjugation under fundamentalist Islamic regimes. Ethnic Serbs have attempted to purge Muslims from Bosnia. Brahmans have kept untouchables in squalid poverty in India.

As God's people, we know these kinds of injustices are prejudiced, inhumane and wrong. Knowing and sharing the Father's heart as we do for all the people He created, we bear the responsibility to cry out in prayer for the poor and the oppressed. It is our privilege to intercede on behalf of the lowest, neediest and most defenseless—to stimulate the Holy Spirit's activity in ministering God's great love to the people who know love the least.

Prayers for justice come easily when you see people being treated unjustly, which is why it is imperative to get out, be informed and see what's going on in the world. Know people. Look out for the unloved and love them. Learn how to pray for the oppressed by befriending them. Years ago, after some acts of anti-Semitism occurred in our city, the members of New Life Church dedicated themselves to honoring and protecting the Jewish community of Colorado Springs. I told the leading rabbi in our area that if ever there were Jews who were prosecuted, slandered, abused or otherwise treated unjustly, New Life Church would be there to defend them. We publicly announced that Christians would use all their resources to ensure the safety, security and happiness of our Jewish citizens. Our support of our Jewish brothers and sisters squelched anti-Semitism, and there hasn't been a reported incident since.

But in order to work for social justice, we must have courage and be willing to sacrifice our resources for the sake of others. When Paul addressed the use of money, he said, "You will be made rich in every way so that you can be generous on every occasion, and through us your generosity will result in thanksgiving to God" (2 Cor. 9:11). This indicates God's desire to prosper his people with resources if they will use them to help others. Let there be no doubt—concern for the oppressed is a major concern for every believer.

Pray the above prayer once again, asking God truly to impart His concern for justice on the earth. Then, as you read the paper, go to work or school and go about the business of your day, intercede on behalf of the mistreated, asking that God's will be done and His kingdom come in their situation.

Praying God's Word

Our desire is . . . that there might be equality. At the present time your plenty will supply what they need, so that in turn their plenty will supply what you need. Then there will be equality (2 Cor. 8:13-14).

You are all sons of God through faith in Christ Jesus. . . . There is neither Jew nor Greek, slave nor free, male nor female, for you are all one in Christ Jesus. If you belong to Christ, then you are Abraham's seed, and heirs according to the promise (Gal. 3:26-29).

SOARING
THROUGH
HUMILITY

Father, I thank You so much for Your grace. You are everything
that I need. I am totally dependent on You. Everything that I
have is a gift from You: my strengths, talents, gifts and abilities
are all from You. Everything I possess is Yours. I acknowledge
Your Lordship in my life. I want You to be supreme.

> *Lord, I give myself to You again. You are the potter; let me*
be clay in Your hands. Make me like You, Father. Cause me to
bring You glory and joy. I surrender to You. O God, I am Yours!

Do you remember your high school? It seems like every student
in my high school fell in one of two categories: overly confident
to the point of arrogance; or devastatingly insecure, afraid to
even look at themselves in the mirror. Doesn't the world sometimes seem like a mix of people who are either too proud or too
timid? Perhaps that's an exaggeration, but many of the people I
counsel from week to week are struggling to find the balance
between arrogance and low self-esteem. Both problems are
equally difficult; but really, pride and insecurity are two sides of
the same coin: a preoccupation with oneself.

As Christians, we don't need to succumb to either extreme.
The worship leader at New Life Church, Ross Parsley, likes to say

that humility is having an accurate view of how God sees you. We know that without Christ, we are wretched, fallen beings. Yet we are extremely valuable to God, valuable enough for Him to give His life for us. In Christ, we can do all things—we are more than conquerors, clothed in the righteousness of God. See the balance? Apart from Him, we can do nothing; with Him, we are champions. This is the crux of Christian humility: a total dependence upon God.

God is the reason we are alive. He is the reason we have this joy and freedom of new life. He is our source: "For in him we live and move and have our being" (Acts 17:28). He is the one that we glorify. Romans 11:36 sums it up beautifully: "For from him and through him and to him are all things." And coming to the realization that everything we have and are is from God should make us stand in awe and humility before Him.

All throughout the Scriptures, God declares His blessing over the humble: "'Has not my hand made all these things, and so they came into being?' declares the LORD. 'This is the one I esteem: he who is humble and contrite in spirit, and trembles at my word'" (Isa. 66:2). God, who made all things, who is exalted above everything and everyone, looks with favor on the humble.

Further, James reminds us that God "opposes the proud but gives grace to the humble" (Jas. 4:6). Can you imagine being opposed by God? Blocked at every turn, resisted and refused by God Himself—what a terrible way to live! But when we humble ourselves, we receive God's grace: His help, His favor, everything we need. Humility is the key that opens the door to God's work in our lives.

Remember that we are clay in the hands of a masterful potter. It is not for us to demand what we want to be or how we should be used. The clay cannot turn itself into anything; if it worries or frets, it cannot alter the process. Actually, realizing that God is in charge is a great relief. It is not our responsibility to mold ourselves or make ourselves better; there is nothing we can do on our own. It is for God to shape us, to direct us and to correct us; and for us to be pliable, yielding to His work, trusting that He knows best.

One of the best ways to keep a humble heart is to be grateful. Gratefulness toward others helps us remember that they are part of the reason we are where we are today. Every great man or woman stands on the shoulders of countless other great men and women. Success is never really achieved alone; it is inevitably the result of some team effort. The heritage given to us by our parents; the deposit placed in us by teachers, youth pastors and other mentors; the encouragement of our friends and family; the hard work of our colleagues—these are all reasons to be grateful to the people in our lives. I tell you, it's hard to become arrogant when you realize how much others have done for you!

Begin to thank God for everything He has done in your life. Think of specific instances. Then thank Him for all the people who have poured themselves into your life over the years and who continue to do so. Name them. Go back to the beginning of this chapter to pray the prayer again, and then move on to the next prayer.

Praying God's Word

I tell you the truth, unless you change and become like little children, you will never enter the kingdom of heaven. Therefore, whoever humbles himself like this child is the greatest in the kingdom of heaven (Matt. 18:3-4).

For in him we live and move and have our being (Acts 17:28).

Prayer 22

SOARING
THROUGH
AUTHORITY

Heavenly Father, I ask You to increase my spiritual authority. Even as You gave Your disciples authority when You sent them out to minister to people, so now please do the same with me. Jesus, I want to go out in the authority of Your name. I believe that in Your name I will do greater things even than You Yourself did (see John 14:12).

Teach me, Lord, about the power of Your name. I want to be Your ambassador, to do Your work here in the world, so I need You to delegate Your authority to me. I never want to abuse this role. Allow me to know You in a more personal way so that it pleases You to give me more and more assignments. I want to be a person that You trust, Father. Help me, too, to lead in my home and business with a servant's heart. I want You to be pleased when You look over Your ranks of workers and see me. I want to be Your friend, and I want it to please You to give me more and more spiritual authority in order to serve Your people.

A right understanding of God's system of authority is vital to living a powerful and victorious life in Christ. According to God's plan, we are all *empowered* with authority in certain areas and *submitted* to authority in others. Remember the centurion in

Matthew 8? He asks Jesus to work a miracle in the life of his paralyzed servant. Jesus agrees to go to the man's house to pray for the servant. The centurion responds:

> Lord, I do not deserve to have you come under my roof. But just say the word, and my servant will be healed. For I myself am a man under authority, with soldiers under me. I tell this one, "Go," and he goes; and that one, "Come," and he comes. I say to my servant, "Do this," and he does it (Matt. 8:8-9).

This officer has it figured out. He is, on the one hand, empowered with authority—he holds command over the soldiers in his unit—and, on the other hand, submitted to authority—he recognizes and defers to Jesus' spiritual leadership.

A few chapters ago, we addressed praying for people in authority over us. Now we are focusing on praying for our own authority—that which God entrusts to us to exercise over others. In the same way that a president delegates responsibility to his cabinet members, God entrusts different areas of His work to different people. Just before His death, Jesus told his disciples, "I tell you the truth, anyone who has faith in me will do what I have been doing. He will do even greater things than these. . . . And I will do whatever you ask in my name" (John 14:12-13). Notice what criteria He gives for sharing in His work and His power: anyone who has faith. To that person He gives the authority to operate in His name.

But beware of using His name without faith! Luke, the author of Acts, records a time when seven sons of a Jewish chief priest were going about casting out devils. They would pray, "In the name of Jesus, whom Paul preaches, I command you to come out" (Acts 19:13). Finally, one of the demons they tried to cast out of someone spoke back to them: "Jesus I know, and I know about Paul, but who are you?" (Acts 19:15). Then the man with the evil spirit pounced on them and gave them all a hearty thrashing (see Acts 19:16). But for those who truly have faith in Jesus, God delegates His work on Earth and shares the power that is available through the use of His name.

God's delegated spiritual authority can be subdivided into what you might call *ministry authority* and *practical authority*. Ministry authority is that which Jesus gave His disciples as they prepared to embark on their ministry journeys (see Mark 6:7). It furnishes the power to heal the sick, cast out demons and proclaim the Gospel with boldness. This is, of course, why we as New Testament believers pray "in Jesus' name." You and I alone don't have the ability to heal anybody. We can't raise the dead and we're powerless against the forces of the enemy. Through Christ, though, the Bible says we can do all things (see Phil. 4:13). So when we pray in Jesus' name, we are really stating our credentials to minister with His delegated authority.

Practical authority is the oversight responsibility God gives us in order to serve those under us in our homes, workplaces and government systems. Husbands are placed in authority over their wives in order to lead them, protect them, encourage them—*to serve them*. God gives children to parents to train them, guide them, provide for them—*to serve them*. Government officials are elected from among the people and by the people—*to serve them*.

Before moving on to the next chapter, take time to pray through the areas of authority that God has delegated to you. Ask Him for more ministry authority to serve people and for more wisdom and compassion in exercising the practical authority He has entrusted to you. Then move on to the next prayer.

Praying God's Word

I tell you the truth, anyone who has faith in me will do what I have been doing. He will do even greater things than these. . . . And I will do whatever you ask in my name (John 14:12-13).

I can do everything through [Christ] who gives me strength (Phil. 4:13).

SOARING THROUGH PERSONAL PURITY

Father, I thank You that the blood of Jesus cleanses me from all sin and unrighteousness. Right now I confess (name the sin). It is wrong and totally evil. I have sinned against You. I repent and turn away from it completely. I choose to hate this sin. I ask You to come and wash me clean, Lord. Make me new again. Give me a pure heart that I might see You. Thank You, Jesus, for Your forgiveness. Help me to live in innocence and purity. I don't ever want to embarrass my family and those I love. I don't ever want to dishonor You. I thank You for Your grace that not only forgives but also empowers me to live in victory.

In over two decades of ministry, I have been privileged to witness wonderful things in the kingdom of God. I have seen people moved with deep conviction and touched by great power. I know many pastors, parachurch ministers and lay leaders who, by the power of the Holy Spirit, have lived lives of integrity and devotion. They are not perfect people, but they are godly, committed servants who have learned how to live clean lives.

Yet over the years I have also seen many tragedies in the Body of Christ. I witnessed men and women who had been mightily used by God fall to temptation, embarrassing their families and ruining their lives. It used to puzzle me how people with such a great anointing on their lives could make such terrible mistakes. As I grew in the Lord, I began to realize that a calling from God is not proof of personal purity. Just because God is using you does not mean that He approves of every aspect of your behavior.

Think of the story of Moses in Numbers 20. He clearly disobeyed God by hitting the rock, instead of speaking to it. We know how serious a mistake this was by the severity of the consequences that followed: Moses was not allowed to enter the Promised Land—the land to which he had been leading the Israelites for over 40 years! Note, however, that God made water come out of the rock in spite of Moses' disobedience. Why? For the sake of the millions of thirsty people! Sometimes God uses us, not because we are right, but because He wants to meet the needs of His people.

But although those we lead may not suffer for our failings, we do: The price for a lack of personal purity is an eroded relationship with God. Christ makes it clear how essential purity is to a right relationship with Him: "Blessed are the pure in heart, for they will see God" (Matt. 5:8). When our hearts are clean, we have the joy of experiencing a wonderful, meaningful personal relationship with God. Every day is another chance to draw near and see a different facet of His beauty. I am convinced: people with pure hearts live better lives! Actually, one of the things I look for in a staff member is innocence. I love it when a person is not full of malice or unforgiveness or is not wrestling with secret sin. You can tell just by their countenance—they are wonderful people to be around.

So the question is, How can we live with purity? The Bible gives us a few keys. First of all, Psalm 119:9 says, "How can a young man keep his way pure? By living according to your word." This is the first step: making the Bible a part of your life. Read it, memorize it, pray it; let God's Word become part of you. It is living and powerful.

Second, confess your sins to God. We are all going to make mistakes; the real issue is how we handle them. First John 1:9

says, "If we confess our sins, he is faithful and just and will for-give us our sins and purify us from all unrighteousness." We must not run from God when we fail; we must run to Him, with godly sorrow and repentance.

The third big idea is that we confess our sins to someone close to us—a friend or our spouse. I don't mean a public decla-ration of our shortcomings; I mean confession in the security of a trusted and loving friend. Most people know 1 John 1:9 and are okay with confessing their sins to God. But a lot of people miss James 5:16, which says, "Therefore confess your sins to each other and pray f or each other so that you may be healed." Confession to God brings forgiveness; confession to each other brings healing. I am a firm believer in living as if there were no such thing as a secret. If we hide our sins and live in darkness, we will never get the healing we so desperately need; in fact, if it is hidden so well that we don't even recognize it, we may never even find forgiveness. The apostle John gives this admonishment: "But if we walk in the light, as he is in the light, we have fellow-ship with one another, and the blood of Jesus, his Son, purifies us from all sin" (1 John 1:7). Walking in the light means living with no secrets. Having fellowship with one another means con-fessing our sins to each other and praying for each other. Trusting the blood of Jesus to cleanse and purify us means con-fessing our sins to God.

All of us have strengths and weaknesses. The goal is to admit when we fail, surrender our lives to God and allow Him to puri-fy us and use our strengths to His glory. Being in good, loving relationships with other people helps us along this path. Pray the prayer above again, asking God to help you to live with puri-ty, and then move on to the next prayer.

PRAYING GOD'S WORD

Blessed are the pure in heart, for they will see God (Matt. 5:8).

Therefore confess your sins to each other and pray for each other so that you may be healed (Jas. 5:16).

If we confess our sins, he is faithful and just and will forgive us our sins and purify us from all unrighteousness (1 John 1:9).

ARRIVING PRAYERS

Going Deeper in the
Christian Life

ARRIVING BY PRAYER AND FASTING

Father, I want more intimacy with You. I want more power in my life. I am so thankful and grateful for all that You have done, and I want to know You more. I commit myself now to a time of prayer and fasting. As I abstain from food, I pray that You would nourish me spiritually. With every hunger pang I want to remember that I am growing in a relationship with You. I pray that during this time You would reveal Yourself to me like never before, helping me to grow in the fruit and gifts of the Spirit. Teach me how to pray in this time. Intercede through me, Holy Spirit! Use me for Your work.

I also pray that this time of fasting would help me to become more disciplined in every area of my life. I pray that I would learn to resist temptation more, to be more diligent in seeking You, to love those around me more selflessly. Lord, I surrender myself to You completely. Shape me, mold me, re-create me. I am Yours, God!

Prayer and fasting is absolutely, far and away one of my favorite spiritual tools. Fasting gives me life and power. It helps me to hone in on the plans of God, to hear His voice and to adjust my life in order to please Him. Do I like to fast? No, I hate it. I hate being hungry, and I absolutely love eating big juicy cheeseburgers and vanilla shakes. Mmm. (Sorry.) But, on the other hand, yes, I do love to fast, because I love the results. Nothing gives me more love for God, more insight into His Word, more power to serve Him and more discipline to live for Him than a time of prayer and fasting.

How do you fast? There are lots of ways, and there's no magic formula for a good fast. I'd suggest reading Elmer L. Towns's *Fasting for Spiritual Breakthrough* before starting a fast.[1] And, of course, if you have medical issues or are an expectant mother, a total fast will be out of the question. It's a good idea to consult with your doctor before beginning *any* fast. But there are many partial fasts you can do—you can fast from any number of things. You can fast from sugar, carbohydrates, caffeine, meat or television.

My favorite fast is a three-day total fast. I abstain from food and all drinks except water. I usually try to go away during that time, either to Praise Mountain, a prayer and fasting retreat center in the Colorado mountains near our church, or to the World Prayer Center, which is located on our church campus. For three days I pray, read my Bible and, if I am in a group, fellowship with people. And I sleep—lots and lots of sleep. On a multiple-day fast like that, your body is really able to rest because it isn't working to process food. So a fast has amazing health benefits in addition to the spiritual nourishment.

Fasting is so powerful because it is an incredible act of self-denial. Done humbly and reverently, it will empty you of worry, stress, sin issues and doubt, and fill you with power, creative ideas, faith and strength.

Isaiah 58 talks about true fasting, and I love reading this chapter when I'm on a fast. Here God explains that fasting is not just about humility or self-sacrifice, and unless a fast produces true change and results in increased servanthood and love, it is not a true fast:

Is this the kind of fast I have chosen, only a day for a man to humble himself? Is it only for bowing one's head like a reed and for lying on sackcloth and ashes? Is that what you call a fast, a day acceptable to the LORD? Is not this the kind of fasting I have chosen: to loose the chains of injustice and untie the cords of the yoke, to set the oppressed free and break every yoke? Is it not to share your food with the hungry and to provide the poor wanderer with shelter—when you see the naked, to clothe him, and not to turn away from your own flesh and blood? Then your light will break forth like the dawn, and your healing will quickly appear; then your righteousness will go before you, and the glory of the LORD will be your rear guard. Then you will call, and the LORD will answer; you will cry for help, and he will say: Here am I (Isa. 58:5-9).

Do you see it? Fasting is not just for us—it is for others. If we fast, we don't reward ourselves for it; we use the fast to draw strength from God in order to serve Him with greater power and efficacy.

Learn to develop a lifestyle of fasting. It is not something that you should do once and then never do again. (But trust me—on that first day you'll be thinking that you'll never want to do it again!) Once you taste the powerful results of fasting, I guarantee that you'll want to do it periodically for the rest of your life. Once it becomes part of your lifestyle—something you do every year or quarter year or even every month—you'll begin to grow in God like never before.

PRAYING GOD'S WORD

After fasting forty days and forty nights, [Jesus] was hungry. The tempter came to him and said, "If you are the Son of God, tell these stones to become bread." Jesus answered, "It is written: 'Man does not live on bread along, but on every word that comes from the mouth of God'" (Matt. 4:2-4).

When you fast, do not look somber. . . . But when you fast, . . . wash your face, so that it will not be obvious to men that you are fasting, but only to your Father, who is unseen (Matt. 6:16-18).

Note
1. Elmer Towns, *Fasting for Spiritual Breakthrough* (Ventura, CA: Regal Books, 1996).

ARRIVING BY ABIDING IN HIM

Heavenly Father, I trust You. You are everything to me. You are my master, my redeemer, my friend. Everything I need I can find in You. I thank You again for saving me, for giving me the Holy Spirit and for patiently teaching me how to grow in You. Now, once again, I settle myself in Your presence. This is where I want to stay. I want to abide in You, God. My hope comes only from You. My help comes only from You. I surrender myself to You completely. I love You.

You have come a long way! Just think of this prayer journey that you have taken and are continuing to take. It's amazing to reflect on—you have received salvation and eternal life, learned to love God and others, grown in the power of the Holy Spirit, renounced sins and prayed for prophetic intercession. Through praying these prayers, your heart and mind have been forever changed as you've been molded into the likeness of Christ. Isn't it incredible? Prayer causes God to reach down deep inside of you, recreating you and making you into who He wants you to be. Moreover, it allows Him to use you strategically and powerfully for His work. You may never know the total results of your prayers, but you can trust that extraordinary things have occurred as you've spent time seeking God.

Now keep it up by abiding in God. I firmly believe that as you've taken this prayer journey, you have totally given your life over to Him. Continue to do so every day. Let Him rule your life. Let Him guide your heart. Let Him teach you how to handle others. Let Him teach you how to be a boss and/or employee. Let Him teach you how to be a spouse, brother, sister or child. Let Him protect you, provide for you, instruct you, heal you, forgive you and sanctify you. Let Him. He wants to be your God all the time, so let Him.

The secret to abiding in God lies in knowing that He is the vine and we are His branches. You know that when a branch is cut from a vine or tree, it no longer remains part of the whole. It can no longer bear fruit because it has no source of life. Jesus explained this to His disciples shortly before He was crucified. He said:

I am the true vine, and my Father is the gardener. He cuts off every branch in me that bears no fruit, while every branch that does bear fruit he prunes so that it will be even more fruitful. You are already clean because of the word I have spoken to you. Remain in me, and I will remain in you. No branch can bear fruit by itself; it must remain on the vine. Neither can you bear fruit unless you remain in me (John 15:1-4).

Remaining, or abiding, in God means giving yourself to Him each day. As you know, the cares of the world are distracting. It is easy to fill our days with everything but God. Actually, this is another way in which Satan is crafty. There are times when we want to do just about anything but pray. But if we want to bear fruit, we have to remain on the vine.

I wrote this prayer book for you because I want to encourage you to abide in God. I don't think of these prayers as mere starting points. The outline here is not just for the new Christian; it is for anyone and everyone who wants to abide in God and grow in His power. Everything we need from God we can find in prayer, and though this little book is not exhaustive, the prayers herein can lay a foundation for you to use the rest of your life.

So keep going for it! Don't give up! God loves you, and He is so pleased when you seek Him. Surround yourself with people who encourage you, who challenge you and exhort you to godliness. There is absolutely nothing better in life, nothing worth doing more, than knowing God. He is our creator. He is our Lord. He is our life, and our primary purpose is to give ourselves to Him and His work on Earth.

PRAYING GOD'S WORD

May God himself, the God of peace, sanctify you through and through. May your whole spirit, soul and body be kept blameless at the coming of our Lord Jesus Christ. The one who calls you is faithful and he will do it (1 Thess. 5:23-34).

This is the confidence we have in approaching God: that if we ask anything according to his will, he hears us. And if we know that he hears us—whatever we ask—we know that we have what we have asked of him (1 John 5:14-15).

The end of all things is near. Therefore be clear minded and self-controlled so that you can pray. Above all, love each other deeply, because love covers over a multitude of sins (1 Pet. 4:7-8).

Draw Closer to God with Prayer

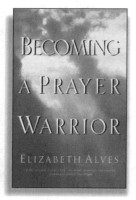

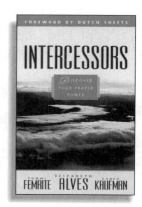
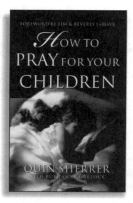

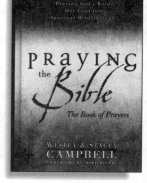